# FREEDOM OF THOUGHT
# AND SOCIETAL FORCES

RUDOLF STEINER (1913)

# FREEDOM OF THOUGHT
# AND SOCIETAL FORCES

## Implementing the Demands
## of Modern Society

Six Lectures Held in Ulm, Berlin, and Stuttgart
May 26–December 30, 1919

TRANSLATED BY CATHERINE E. CREEGER

INTRODUCTION BY CHRISTOPHER BAMFORD

# RUDOLF STEINER

SteinerBooks

CW 333

SteinerBooks

Anthroposophic Press

610 Main Street
Great Barrington, Massachusetts 01230
www.steinerbooks.org

Translation from the German by Catherine E. Creeger

This book is volume 333 in the Collected Works (CW) of Rudolf Steiner, published
by SteinerBooks, 2008. It is a translation of *Gedankenfreiheit und soziale Kräfte*,
second edition, published by Rudolf Steiner Verlag, Dornach, Switzerland, 1985.


Library of Congress Cataloging-in-Publication Data

Steiner, Rudolf, 1861-1925.
  [Gedankenfreiheit und soziale Kräfte. English]
  Freedom of thought and societal forces : implementing the demands of
modern society : six public lectures given in Ulm, Berlin and Stuttgart, May
26-December 30, 1919 / Rudolf Steiner ; translated by Catherine E. Creeger ;
introduction by Christopher Bamford.
      p. cm. — (The collected works of Rudolf Steiner ; v. 333)
  Includes bibliographical references and index.
  ISBN 978-0-88010-597-2
  1. Liberty. 2. Social psychology. 3. Social history. I. Title.
  JC571.S78813 2008
  323.44–dc22
                              2008034373

Printed in the United States

# CONTENTS

# INTRODUCTION

CHRISTOPHER BAMFORD

On February 27, 1919, a couple of months before the public lectures collected here were given between May and December, Rudolf Steiner celebrated his fifty-eighth birthday. Three months before that, on November 11, 1918, World War I—with its unimaginable, senseless suffering and bloodshed, almost ten million dying, six thousand a day, for fifteen hundred days—finally limped to its unhappy conclusion. The armistice and the subsequent Peace Treaty, deceitfully finagled at Versailles, would humiliate Germany with devastating demands for reparations. Central Europe was left in tatters. Confidence in its culture and itself had evaporated. What had been apparent bourgeois solidity was revealed to be a house of cards. Deep, widespread social, economic, and political confusion was pervasive. From all sides and at every level the state—since Hegel and Bismarck a bulwark against barbarianism—found itself threatened, and now the barbarians were at the gates. Revolutionaries, thugs, as well as intellectuals, from both right and left, fomented an endless stream of social conflicts. Among its many other consequences, the Russian Revolution's success in 1917 had empowered and radicalized socialists and Marxists of all persuasions. Whatever their differences, they were united in calling for an end to the socio-economic divide between owners and workers, rich and poor, which, they believed with some justification, had sustained the untenable conditions that had led to the war in the first place. At the same time, from the right, traumatized by the shame of defeat, disaffected patriots, lovers of "old Germany," and alienated forerunners of National Socialism were blindly striking out, reacting to every turn in the political situation with random street violence, and already hatching unrealizable dreams of a German return to power, a "third Reich." It cannot have been an easy time.

Nevertheless, for Rudolf Steiner and his near-miraculous shepherd-ing into being of Anthroposophy, 1919 was an extraordinary year of transformation and the beginnings of new cultural impulses that, over the next few years remaining to him until his death in 1925, would give the world new forms of social thinking, pedagogy, medicine, pharmacology, agriculture, art, and religion: initiatives that still have the possibility of transforming human life and earthly evolution. Much of that program lay ahead. But a start was being made—on three fronts. First, the year was dedicated to the promotion—the social and political work—of a radically new way of organizing soci-ety and social, economic, juridical, and cultural relations. He called it "the threefolding of the social organism." In this he was, as always, responding to the needs of his time, to the precise point or fulcrum where, as the instrument of the spiritual world, he could make the greatest contribution to humanity's development. Besides "threefold-ing," and perhaps more importantly, at least in terms of its immediate and continuing success, 1919 also saw the creation of Waldorf peda-gogy and the founding of the first Waldorf school under the auspices of Emil Molt's Waldorf Astoria cigarette factory in Stuttgart. Lastly, eurythmy—developed over the preceding seven years—was unveiled during this period as a new art form with public performances in eight cities.

The seeds of this new "springtime" for Anthroposophy were sown in 1917, the year in which the new geo-political map of the twenti-eth century was being re-drawn. In Russia, the Bolshevik Revolution marked the beginning of Soviet power in the East, while, from the West, the entry of the United States into the war announced its pres-ence as a new global world power. As a result, between Lenin and Woodrow Wilson, central Europe found itself trapped in a new kind of meta-war of extreme propaganda. Meanwhile, as the ideological drama developed, the inevitable material outcome of the war was becoming increasingly clear. Only the timing remained unknown.

Such was the context in which Rudolf Steiner was asked for counsel—essentially, what should be done when the Peace finally came—by Otto von Lerchenfeld, a highly placed German career diplomat; soon, an Austrian counterpart (and Anthroposophist),

Ludwig von Poltzer-Hoditz joined in their discussions. Working with these two partners—at great speed and with a deep sense of responsibility—Steiner formulated what he saw as a solution to the social contradictions and fundamental misapprehension of reality that had led Europe to the civilizational cul-de-sac of the Great War. Recognizing the inherent flaw in the unitary state, he proposed the separation—or "threefolding"—of social life into three independent, autonomous, but interrelated areas, each with its own organizing principle: namely, 1. An autonomous cultural life, arising out of the freedom of individual human beings; 2. Equality and justice in the sphere of legal rights, arising from the juridical equality of all human beings; 3. An understanding of economics that was cooperative and associative—brotherly-and-sisterly—rather than competitive as in the free-market system of capitalism. These ideas were then presented in the form of a Memorandum as a path to social and cultural renewal appropriate to the historical moment in which central Europe found itself. The Memorandum was then distributed to leading politicians in Germany and Austria. Unfortunately, however, as is so often the case with such initiatives, nothing came of the proposal at the time. Yet it was not something Steiner proposed idly. On the contrary, he believed fervently in its rightness and necessity for our time. Therefore he continued to work on it. In 1919, with the termination of hostilities, it became a central focus of his endeavors.

Here it must be remembered that Steiner's social activism was not new. While it had never before been his primary concern in such a direct way, he came to it fully prepared. To begin with, he was a working-class child, a scholarship boy, who had to support himself all his life. As such, he had a "common touch" and always felt at ease with ordinary people. While his philosophical path certainly led him to the epistemological, as well as ethical, monism and Christian realism ("Not I but the Christ in me") of *The Philosophy of Freedom* and ultimately to the mystical moment of witnessing the Mystery of Golgotha in a "festival of insight," at the same time it took important detours through the radically free terrain opened up by Friedrich Nietzsche and Max Stirner. From this period of his life, he inherited a deep distaste for what he considered the pernicious materialism and hypocrisy of the bourgeoisie. Indeed, it might be said that Steiner was always a radical, and always concerned with social questions. Before the turn of the century and extending into his first years as a spiritual teacher (1897-1904, at least), we see him not only passing through an "anarchist" period and participating in many radical cultural societies, but also, most importantly, enjoying a seven-year teaching position at the Worker's College that was founded by Wilhelm Liebknecht. The depth of his commitment to social issues is indicated by the fact that in 1902, just before the founding of the German Section of the Theosophical Society, Steiner shared the stage with Rosa Luxemburg. Of this occasion, he said much later (in 1919):

> I once stood in Spandau on the same lecture platform as Rosa Luxemburg, who has just met so tragic an end. [She had just been murdered, that is, assassinated.] We were both speakers at a gathering of the proletariat, where the theme was science and the workers. From Rosa Luxemburg's words one could see how inspirationally she could work into the souls of these working-class people, who had come on a Sunday afternoon with their wives and children. It was a heart-warming gathering. (CW 329, not translated)

Social concerns were thus not new to Rudolf Steiner. In fact, already in 1905, in an article in *Luzifer-Gnosis* entitled "Spiritual Science and the Social Question" (not translated, CW 34) he had already intimated a "threefold" solution.

Social threefolding, however, was not the only seed planted in 1917. Related, and equally important, especially for what in its turn would become the anthropological basis of Waldorf pedagogy, was Steiner's finding himself in the fall of 1917 finally able to articulate the three-fold nature of the human being. He had been working on this idea since about 1882, when he was only twenty-one; but it was not until 1917, in a lecture and in an appendix to *Riddles of the Soul* (CW 21) that he was first able to articulate it to his satisfaction completely and fully. Without this profound insight into the threefold constitution of the human being, as Steiner related at a public lecture in Bern two years later (March 11, 1919), he would not have come to the idea of the importance of social threefolding:

> I do not believe that I would have come to a true understand-ing of the idea of the threefold nature of the social organism or body if I had not previously undertaken research into the human organism itself—research on which I reported at least in outline in my book *Riddles of the Soul*. In it, I showed that the ordinary, natural human organism is of a threefold nature—namely, that this natural human organism is threefold in its differentiation into a sense-and-nerve organism, a rhythmical (circulatory) organism, and a metabolic organism. To recognize these three members of the natural human organism is vitally important for contemporary human thinking. For it is by means of the kind of thinking and insight that we can exercise in connection with this view that we come to true insight into the social organism itself in its threefold nature.

Less significantly perhaps in the short term—yet not hopefully in the long term—1917 also saw Steiner turning to the need for Anthroposophy to participate in the renewal of higher education. Anthroposophy's mission to transform the academic sciences would in fact become a dominant theme of Steiner's lectures to the so-called youth movement during the last few years of his life (1922-1924), but the ripe fruit of that aspiration still lies ahead of us.

The seeds thus planted, the soil had to be made ready. Thus, in preparation for the end of the war, when cultural-spiritual renewal and transformation would become possible again, Steiner reissued—with additions, re-workings, and changes—his foundational writ-ten works: *Intuitive Thinking as a Spiritual Path* (*The Philosophy of Freedom* CW 4), *Goethe's Worldview* (CW 6), *Theosophy* (CW 9), *How to Know Higher Worlds* (CW 10), *Goethe's Spiritual Path as Revealed in Faust and the Fairy Tale of The Green Snake and the Beautiful Lily* (CW 22), *A Way of Self-Knowledge* and *The Threshold of the Spiritual World* (CW 16/17), and *Riddles of Philosophy* (CW 18). This task, by itself, must have taken an almost unimaginable amount of work and concentration. But that was not all. In addition, Steiner also worked on a new edition of *An Outline of Esoteric Science* (which would not appear until 1920), wrote an introduction to *The Mission of Folk Souls* (CW 121), and gave lectures on "Historical Symptomology" (CW 185) and "The Developmental Foundations for the Development of Social Judgment" (CW 185a). In this way, indefatigably, Steiner prepared the ground for the following year—1919, the year of three-folding, the creation of Waldorf education, and the public manifestation of eurythmy.

Until April, Steiner remained in Switzerland, lecturing on the idea of threefolding in Zurich, Basel, Berne, and Winterthur. On the basis of these lectures, in order to introduce threefolding to a wider public he then wrote the short book *Social Renewal* (CW 23). Following this, he traveled to Germany, where things were naturally much more unsettled. Already in February, in collaboration with his coworkers, he had issued "A Call to the German People and the Cultural World," which was underwritten by several well-known personalities of the time and appeared in many leading newspapers. In it, Steiner spoke of the history that had led to the present moment and called "for a broader understanding of life" which would strive "with strong thinking to understand the evolutionary forces of modern humanity…and devote itself with courageous determination to the unfolding of these forces." In Germany, he sought above all to address businesses— workers, management, and owners—trying to inspire on all sides a collegial, associative approach to their enterprises. He spoke of creating "business councils" and creating "cultural councils." Despite his throwing his whole being into it, and lecturing tirelessly, the response, though not completely negligible was too small to effect any change. As for members of the bourgeoisie or middle class, they remained unimpressed and passive. By midsummer, then, Steiner turned his attention to the new (first) Waldorf School. Later in the year, he returned to the threefold theme, writing articles and giving a public lecture cycle on *The Social Future* (GA 332a).

*Freedom of Thought and Societal Forces*, containing six public lectures given between May and December 1919, provides us with a broad, accessible overview of—or a kind of general introduction or background to—Steiner's social thinking during this first period of his social activism. Readers may be surprised at his radical ability to meet social reality without prejudice or preconception and fearlessly describe what he sees. He understood that any such description, at least in his time, must acknowledge that—although perhaps only symptomatic in a larger sense—the demands for changes in the social order derived above all from ordinary members of the working class, for it was they who, then (and probably still today) experienced most directly the inequities and hypocrisies of the system. In other words, Steiner could sympathize with the reality that, as a result of indus-trialization and "soul-destroying capitalism," working-class people found themselves forced into a life almost exclusively dominated by economic activity—i.e., living only to work for the pittance that enabled them to survive. Their labor—the labor of many—supported the few: no question of that. Hence they thought the solution to their problem was purely economic. But, from Steiner's point of view, real-ity was not so simple: the underlying issue was spiritual or cultural.

In truth, it is not just the poor who demand some sort of economic and social equity: the demand is human; it is an evolutionary and soci-etal call—which the upper classes, who could have, failed to answer. Indeed, culture as a whole has failed to respond. It is Steiner's point that both culture and the cultured classes have become progressively estranged from "real life," and from the lives of ordinary people. Ordinary people look at culture and education and see them only reinforcing the status quo, something not for them, and by no means as agents of change. Thus the issue is not simply a more equitable distribution of wealth. Rather, it has to do with the creation of a culture that will bring people together in creative, harmonious ways rather than segmenting them economically and promoting only the financial-cultural interests of the elites (corporate or intellectual). One of the great illusions, Steiner says, is "that we can convey the culture of an exclusive minority to the masses." On the contrary, our time demands a culture that includes all social classes. Thus, "the first prerequisite for a healthy social life is a cultural and intellectual life that is allowed to develop on the basis of its own intrinsic values"—a free cultural life.

While the general evolution of social consciousness—through its natural democratic tendency—is now beginning to make legal individual and human rights universal, the economic question still remains muddied mostly because, as Steiner sees it, it subsumes two things, labor and capital, that do not belong to it. For Steiner, the circulation of goods alone constitutes what we call the "economy," and not what is usually subsumed under it: labor and capital. In the modern economy, labor has become a commodity, which condemns workers to a life reduced to work. But labor cannot be priced like a commodity; it needs to be extricated from the economic process, which must become autonomous and self-governing and concerned only with the circulation and value of goods. For Steiner, the only way to accomplish the shift would be to establish the independence of labor from the economy. Labor should be shifted to the sphere of rights, the only place where the freedom that workers seek is to be found. Similarly, capital must be liberated from egotistic ownership and allowed—like goods—simply to circulate. It should be only a placeholder for goods, and like goods should be allowed to circulate, gradually wear out, and then disappear. All these are radical proposals, but in these lectures Steiner makes a convincing case for their feasibility and relevance.

He is clear, however, that economic and social realities cannot be separated from the spiritual realities of human existence. From Steiner's point of view, humanity today suffers primarily from a lack of self-knowledge of the human as a spiritual being. Thinking has become useless—abstract, automatic—because everything related to the human being as a whole has been eliminated from it. To remedy this situation, the first step is to admit it and develop an inner attitude of modesty and humility that acknowledges the inadequacy of ordinary thinking to approach such questions. Second, we must increase our capacity to love—to love one another and the world. This, though often overlooked, is fundamental. Without an enhanced and growing love, any other capacities we might gain will remain arid and unprofitable. But on the basis of these two prerequisites—modesty and love—we can begin a path of inner work that will allow us to truly understand reality differently and more deeply. The second lecture thus describes in some detail with fascinating commentary various soul and spirit meditative practices that anyone can do. It makes clear that without such inner work, and so without spiritual self-knowledge, no real social progress is possible.

Approaching the same reality from another side, we can easily see that what ails our individual ordinary thinking is the same as what ails our culture in general. It, too, has become increasingly abstract, automatic, elitist, and removed from reality. Culture, like thinking, must become alive and universally human. Here Steiner speaks from his own experience at the Worker's College, where he could speak about anything if he spoke in a living way about what he had made his own. But when he had to "do the fashionable thing" and take them to museums and other places where "bourgeois culture" was on display, the gap between their intellectual and spiritual longings and what they were presented with was nearly unbridgeable. As Steiner says: "We understand art, science, and religion only when they are based on the shared perceptions of our peers—not when there is a rift between those who are supposed to enjoy culture and those who actually can. We experienced this discrepancy as a profound cultural lie…" Education, culture must become the free expression through free individuals of the universal whole to which all have access equally, not the product of the "surplus" value that privileges some members of society at the expense of others. Here, above all, we see the importance of education, and are given a different kind of lens through which to view the Waldorf movement, which is an attempt to develop pedagogy out of the human being itself—the universal human.

None of what Steiner is talking about, however, is possible if human beings do not develop what he calls "freedom of thought." To develop such freedom is one purpose of spiritual science. The gift of humanity's present evolutionary moment, which Steiner calls "the consciousness soul," freedom of thought, means thinking, feeling and acting out of one's own direct connection to the spirit. It is the fruit both of living, non-dualistic meditative thinking beyond all determination and habit—whether psychological, physical, or logical—and "true, devoted love for the object of one's actions." Overcoming egotism, authentic freedom of thought is always ethical. Directed toward the world, out of the spirit, it acts solely out of love of the deed: just so. We may call it intuition—but intuition becomes real only when acted upon or embodied. Freedom, intuition of this kind, furthermore, only becomes possible through the recognition of our immortality, as Dostoevsky did when he asserted that, without the conviction of the immortality of the soul, the love of one's neighbor—loving one another as Christ loved us, which is the new commandment—is impossible. Therefore, as Steiner says, "social forces, freedom of thought, and spiritual science are all related."

Were it to become more general, such exercise of freedom of thought, as Steiner conceives of it, would provide a safe way out of the twinned dangers of materialism and abstraction, which threaten social life both in the narrower sense of "national" life, but also in the broader, more global, geopolitical sense. In place of materialistic, egotistic thinking, one consequence of which is clearly modern warfare and the material use of force generally, freedom of thought opens a way to act and know—lovingly—out of the spirit; instead of abstraction, which only exacerbates materialism and materialistic action divorced from reality, freedom of thought promotes concrete, realistic, context-specific responsibility.

As the fifth lecture printed here makes clear: this path is none other than that made possible for all humanity by Christ's deed on Golgotha, *but embodied in a new way*. Steiner's mission is to hasten the new embodiment:

> We will derive truly socially responsible views only from sources that also feed our modern supersensible activity. Viewpoints derived from a merely mechanistic view of nature are liabilities, as are lifeless copies of centuries-old religious denominations that have lost their vitality. Now, more than at any other time, humankind needs the power of the Christ, but we need a new way to find him. All of the old ways, whether obvious or disguised, belong in the liability column…. What we really need, however, is spiritual deepening that can truly make inroads into our material life and accompany it every step of the way. My ongoing mission is to describe a spiritual view of life complete

with ideas that can shape actions and soul-forces that can generate morality and religious reverence.

In other words, as Steiner puts it in the final lecture: "Without spirit cognition, our ethical impulses on behalf of Western culture are totally unfounded." Caught between virtually empty religious views disconnected from individual spiritual perception and prescriptions cobbled together from half or misunderstood opinions based in the natural sciences, we are called to make the world new out of spiritual insight, "warmed and enthused," in Steiner's words, "by a soul-spiritual element." This is the real spiritual need of our times to which Anthroposophy seeks to respond. Thus Steiner concludes these lectures with these inspiring words filled with great courage and determination:

> In the face of all resistance and to the best of its ability, anthroposophical spiritual science must continue to stand for knowledge that supports our actions, our ethical and social endeavors, and the finest human hopes. Our opponents may succeed in muzzling spiritual science, but as soon as it regains even the slightest freedom, it will resume speaking out about the truth it recognizes as necessary for humanity. When the tide began turning in favor of the Allies, the Goetheanum was there for the whole world to see, as testimony to an international culture unapologetically based on further development of a Goethean approach rooted in Germanic culture. Similarly, in spite of all obstacles, anthroposophical spiritual science will continue to fight for the perceptions and knowledge that shape its convictions. This content, although rooted in Central Europe, belongs to the whole world.

# FREEDOM OF THOUGHT
## AND SOCIETAL FORCES

*Rudolf Steiner*

# 1

## The Threefold Aspect
## of the Societal and Class Question

Here, as elsewhere in Württemberg and Switzerland, I will address the most incisive and important question of modern times in connection with the recently issued "Appeal to the German People and Culture." Most of you will have seen this appeal, which argued for a threefold subdivision of the body social. A complete exposition of its contents is available in my little book *Toward Social Renewal*,[†] but please allow me to fill in a few of the details for you tonight.

Since the shattering events of the recent catastrophic World War, societal issues that actually date back to the mid-1800s have appeared in a completely new guise. These issues should be obvious to all human souls who are alert to the signs of the times. If we compare this historical tidal wave with its previous manifestations, we realize that it has now assumed a completely new form that we cannot afford to ignore.

In the last four or five years, it was often said that this terrible, catastrophic World War was unprecedented in human history. In the ongoing crisis it heralded, however, we heard very little about the need for completely new impulses to transform the social order. Although the need to relearn everything and totally change our ways of thinking is quite obvious, we hear nothing about that. Old thoughts are what led humankind into this terrible catastrophe, and new impulses will have to lead us out of it. Real in-depth observation of the societal demands resonating from increasing numbers of human hearts and minds will lead us to these impulses. These demands can be ignored only by those asleep to the times, who will continue to wait out events until the old edifice collapses into oblivion.

Today we often imagine societal issues to be obvious or even very simple, but if our judgment is based on truly extensive experience of vital present and future needs rather than on murky theories or individual personal demands, we must see these issues as the confluence of multiple forces that have emerged in the course of humanity's development. In a certain sense, these forces carry the seeds of their own destruction within them. To those with a real overview of the circumstances, societal issues present three faces: cultural or spiritual life, judicial or legal life, and economic life. During the nineteenth century and the first two decades of the twentieth, we came to attribute almost all issues and problems in our public life to economics. This lack of clear-sightedness was due to our belief that if we simply manage to get our bearings in the economic sector, everything else will fall into place by itself. Most people today, regardless of whether they lean politically to the right or to the left, fail to see cultural, intellectual, and spiritual activity as an essential aspect of the social order. Consequently, my initial observations tonight will be devoted to that aspect.

Current demands for changes in the social order originate in the rank-and-file of the working class. We will talk later about the three aspects of the trials and tribulations faced by working men and women in the times leading up to present conditions. As a consequence of industrialization, soul-destroying capitalism, and other trappings of modern civilization, the working class has been forced almost exclusively into economic activity. This activity naturally provides the context for working-class demands, which are therefore formulated in economic terms. The issues, however, are not purely economic. Simply by recognizing that old ways of thinking have failed to adequately address the facts, which speak loudly for themselves, we can also recognize that social movements are concerned about more than just economic and legal problems. In fact, the underlying issue is spiritual or cultural.

In large parts of the civilized world, we now confront an increasingly obvious failure of the status quo. Political parties of various persuasions have developed platforms and programs that are now proving inadequate to address the reality of our situation. It is no longer enough to perpetuate old party platforms. We must confront the facts directly, with all due seriousness and with a keen sense of reality.

First of all, let's take a look at the development of the human activity that led to this crisis. Above all, we must look at the deep, virtually unbridgeable cleft between the working and non-working classes. The civilization enjoyed by the latter has been highly praised as a sign of great progress in modern times. Commonplace technologies now quickly deliver people and thoughts around the globe in ways that would once have been derided as utopian visions. We never tire of glorifying this progress. But today we must also add another perspective: we must ask how this progress came about. It is based entirely on an underlying structure made up of broad masses of humanity, of countless individuals whose work makes possible the culture of the few. Now these masses have grown up; they have come to their senses and are demanding their rightful share. If we truly understand this age we live in, we must see the demands of the masses as the great, historical demands of our time itself. We must realize that the call for the socialization of economic life represents not simply the demands of one social class but the demands of humanity itself at this point in history.

The leading classes participating in our much-praised civilization have been conspicuous in their inability to rise to the occasion. They have failed to seize any recent opportunities to bridge the gap between themselves and a working class that is increasingly able to articulate its justified demands. More specifically, the ideas that would have needed to flow into our public life in order to bridge this gap have been lacking. An idiosyncrasy of our much-praised modern culture is that it has become increasingly estranged from real life. Individuals are aware only of the life in their immediate surroundings. Entire groups of people have been unable to derive any all-encompassing, inspiring ideas or ideals from our cultural institutions (specifically, from our education system).

Let me tell you one typical story that could be repeated tens and even hundreds of times from varying perspectives:

> I like to mention the example of Alfred Kolb, a senior civil servant who took his destiny in hand in a most remarkable and admirable way. I say this in all seriousness; I always try to avoid sarcastic comments, and there is clearly no need for them in this instance. At a certain point in his life, Kolb did something that very few civil servants do. Most of them retire and live off their pensions when they have had enough of civil service. Kolb, however, left his post and went to America, where he worked as an ordinary laborer, first in a brewery and then in a bicycle factory. He then wrote a book about his experiences.[†] In a remarkable passage in this book, Kolb says something like this: Formerly, when I passed an unemployed person on the street, I wondered, why isn't that scoundrel working? Now I know differently. I have changed my mind about many other things as well, and I know that even the worst treatment life deals out does not look so bad from the viewpoint of a comfortable study.

This confession is profoundly characteristic of the social circumstances of our time. A product of our culture, a man with many years of human destiny under his belt—at least, as many as it takes to become a senior civil servant—knows nothing about human work and therefore nothing about human life. To learn something about the life he is supposed to "serve" as a member of the leading classes, he has to take his destiny in hand and accept employment as a common laborer. As a result, he acquires a completely different perspective on life.

This example, which is only one among many, shows how estranged the culture of our upper classes has become from the life of the masses. The broad masses of people, needy in body and soul, see firsthand how the leading classes manage the economy and realize that something is wrong. They see that our leading classes are not "leading" the economy in the right spirit. And now the question is: What needs to change?

In many other respects, too, we can see that over the past few centuries, the leading classes have become estranged from everything that could have prevented catastrophe. In upper class circles, people talked very seriously and developed eminently worthy opinions about all sorts of nice subjects—about loving your neighbor and human fraternity and the need to be a good human being—but they had no connection to real life. At best, their deliberations lead to investigations. In the mid-1800s, for example, the English government investigated the management of coalmines; its findings are still pertinent today. People warmed themselves in front of coal fires while discussing human existence and human goodness, progressive morals and advanced culture. These people needed to learn that their coal was mined by poor children as young as nine, eleven, or thirteen—children who almost never saw daylight because they went down into the mines before sunrise and came up only after dark. Many similar examples could be cited. But did such findings motivate the leading classes of humanity to make real changes in the social order? Well, some people will say we have seen many changes for the better, but I would say that any improvement is due not to initiatives on the part of the leading classes, but to the bitter struggle of those who suffered under their leadership.

What must we look at today? We must look at what people who work from morning till night see—from the *outside* only—as they pass our high schools and universities. They know only what they experienced in primary school. They do not know how goals and standards for elementary education are imposed from above. They see only that their elementary schools are not producing today's economic leaders. This is the first face of the societal issue. In spite of all the praise we lavish on the cultural facet of our life (including our education system), it is no match for the tasks and challenges of our time.

Next, let's look at the economy. When workers first began to organize and demand their share, industry leaders often noted dismissively that if everything were divided equally, each person would get very little. After a while, they dropped this objection, because although it is quite true on the one hand, it is very stupid on the other. Recently, we have heard it again, with increasing frequency, but it actually misses the point. If we understand the unique structure of our modern economy, we know that the actual underlying reasons for the physical and psychological hardships endured by the working class are quite different. The cultural aspect of our society has been inadequately developed, and as a consequence we do not understand how to channel the increasing domination of the economy by technology in ways that would permit each individual a humanly worthy existence.

To be sure, it has often been pointed out that the modern workers' movement emerged in reaction to modern technology, machinery, and soul-destroying capitalism. We have forgotten, however, that in our society the cultural domain has been incapable of controlling these factors as they appeared. Why is that the case? As machines, industrialization, and capitalism developed, humanity began to see state take-over of cultural affairs as a major, desirable step forward. Today, any objections to government control of cultural matters still meet with intense criticism. Culturally active people take pride in pointing out the great intellectual progress we have made since the Middle Ages, and it is certainly true that we do not wish to return to the Dark Ages. We need to move forward, not backward. Nonetheless, there is another question that must be raised here. It has been said that during the Middle Ages, intellectual activity in general and science in particular existed only to serve theology or the church. But what does our modern intellectual life serve? Here is another example, again one out of hundreds or thousands, and once again, I am speaking about an individual I admire greatly. In my opinion, this man was a very important scientist.[†] He was also the general secretary of a scholarly society at the vanguard of German intellectual life.[†] In his well-received speeches, he attempted to express what the esteemed members of the Prussian Academy of Sciences considered their greatest honor. (As a historical aside, it should be noted that the Berlin Academy has always been something that sought to express spiritually the impulse of the House of Hohenzollern.) In the eighteenth century, one of the Hohenzollerns had to appoint a president for the Academy—I am not making this up; this is historical fact—and did that institution the great honor of installing his court jester at its head.[†] Nonetheless, this great scholar of the late nineteenth century said that the scholarly gentlemen of the Berlin Academy considered it their greatest honor to be the scientific bodyguards of the Hohenzollerns.†

Such statements must be seen as signs of the times. We must consider what intellectual activity has become through dependence on the power of the state and the related power of capitalism. If our actions are truly motivated by reality—that is, by life's necessities rather than by any preconceived notions—we will realize (contrary to all of the preconceptions of our time) that intellectual activity will come into its own as an independent power only when it is no longer subsumed by state activity, and is thus allowed to rely entirely on itself. Everything that makes up our intellectual life, especially the educational system, must be responsible for its own administration, from the highest offices of cultural affairs to the teachers of the lowest grades. Only the forces inherent in cultural or spiritual activity must be allowed to set the standards for administration of cultural and intellectual matters. Those actively and inwardly involved in this field must be responsible for developing its governing body. It must stand on its own feet.

This is the first face of what we are calling the threefold structure of the healthy social organism. An independent field of cultural or spiritual activity will relate to life very differently than the antisocial cultural/spiritual activity we have gradually fallen into and seemingly feel no need to escape.

We need to hear from individuals with real experience in this field. For years, I taught at the Berlin Workers' School, founded by Liebknecht.† As a result, I know how to draw on sources of cultural and intellectual activity that are available to all instead of being luxuries reserved for the privileged classes. Once found, these sources allow us to speak to all individuals who aspire to a humanly worthy existence for both body and soul. From my practical experience, I know that my working-class students always understood me better when I spoke out of such sources. Because of my students' sense of cultural obligation, so to speak, there were also times when I had to accompany them to museums or other such establishments that did not represent a true folk culture but testified to a culture of the few. I realized then that the schism between classes was also a cultural gap. My students could not really absorb or inwardly participate in outgrowths of the culture of the few. This is a mistake that is still often made today. We think that we are "educating the masses" when we throw them the crumbs of what our universities, high schools, and other institutions of higher learning have cultivated based on the social sensibilities of the few. We go to great lengths to educate adults with our public libraries, community colleges, people's theaters, and so on, but we consistently err in believing that we can convey the culture of an exclusive minority to the masses. We cannot. Our time demands a cultural life that includes all social classes. The development of such a culture, however, requires unity between the producers of culture and its intended participants, along with all their sensibilities and social backgrounds. It is not enough to throw people crumbs. On the cultural level, the entire populace must work as a whole. To make this possible, however, cultural affairs must be freed from governmental and capitalist economic constraints. In one short lecture, I cannot go into great detail about the need to extricate cultural and intellectual institutions—especially the school system— from governmental and economic influences. I cannot even tell you everything that is included in my book *Toward Social Renewal*, but the first prerequisite for the development of a threefold social organism is a cultural and intellectual life that is allowed to develop on the basis of its own intrinsic values.

We need not be afraid of a culture of this sort. Even if we hold a low opinion of human beings in general, we need not fear a general reversion to illiteracy if parents are not legally required to send their children to school. To the contrary, the working class will become increasingly aware of the benefits of education. If working-class children are not obliged to go to school, they will not be kept at home; their parents will send them voluntarily. The proponents of comprehensive schools in particular have nothing to fear: comprehensive schools are the only possible outcome of fostering the independence of cultural institutions.[†]

That is enough for now about the separation of cultural affairs from the state and the economy. The second area of life that we must consider in studying modern social issues is the sphere of rights.

People have talked and written about civil rights from many different perspectives, but if our observations and perceptions about them are based on reality, scholarly definitions make as much sense as "defining" the colors blue and red, which are readily accessible to anyone with normal eyes. Similarly, the rights to which all individuals are entitled simply by virtue of being human are evident to any alert human mind, and the minds of the modern working class are increasingly alert.

In the domain of the law and civil rights, the modern leading classes find themselves in an unpleasant and contradictory situation. On the one hand, the old patriarchal system has become useless to them, and they cannot help but encourage a certain level of democracy. It is in their best interest as capitalists to hire skilled workers with certain mental abilities. Unfortunately for the capitalists, however, encouraging individual faculties of the human mind tends to make other abilities emerge all by themselves. Of course, the leading classes hoped to develop only those abilities that make for skillful factory workers. Concomitantly, however, working-class minds awoke to the circumstances of the old patriarchy and became aware of human rights. They then began to wonder whether the modern nation-state really provides a fertile ground for these rights. Instead of universal human rights, they saw privileged and underprivileged classes; and the result was what we call the class struggle of the working class. Underlying this struggle is nothing more or less than the great and justified demand for a humanly worthy existence for all people.

The rights issue is the second aspect of the class issue, but we cannot become fully aware of its significance without considering the third aspect, namely, the economy. The economy has subsumed two things that really do not belong to it—human labor and capital. Only the circulation of goods actually belongs to the economy.

It seems to me that the events of recent years should have taught us that the workers themselves are the most important factor in the proletarian social movement. Given the current state of affairs, simply listening to lectures about the working class does not equip us to assess the real situation of the working class. We would need to have seen for ourselves how over the decades workers have spent many evening hours, after days of hard work, coming together to learn about the modern economic movement and the significance of labor, capital, and the production and consumption of goods. We would need to have seen for ourselves how the working class hungered for education, while the upper classes went to the theater and devoted themselves to other amusements, perhaps casting a glance from on high at the miserable life of the working class. Meanwhile, the workers were growing and learning and developing a cultural life of their own.

It is a shame that the working-class issue is still being construed as simply a question of bread and hungry stomachs. It is a shame that we have taken so long to realize that all working-class struggles originate with the demand for a humanly worthy life that does not allow either the body or the mind to waste away. But while workers were reflecting on their collective situation and learning about the modern economy, they were also becoming conscious of their individual situations in a life controlled by the upper classes. They were told that history reflected a divine or moral world order, or at least an order based on ideas and ideals; but all they could see was that their work produced the profits that supported upper-class lifestyles. That is why the words of the *Communist Manifesto*[†] resonated so deeply with them and made them conscious of their situation.

In spite of all recent progress, workers are still condemned to let their labor be bought and sold in the market like a commodity. The basis of the working class's demand is the feeling—not always clearly expressed—that it is unworthy of human beings to allow part of themselves to be bought and sold. Entering into a wage relationship means selling one's labor, and the selling of labor belongs to older times. It is a remnant of serfdom. Workers have realized that goods belong in commerce but labor does not. If you take goods to the market, you can sell them and return home with the proceeds, but if you sell your labor, you cannot simply take your money and go home; you have to show up and work. Human beings are forced to follow their labor. That is what the working class experienced as an existence unworthy of human beings.

So now the big question is: what must happen so that labor is no longer a commodity? As a rule, members of the upper classes think very little about labor. They simply open their wallets and pay with big bills. Do they ever think about how much worker's labor those bills represent? Whatever their thoughts on the subject, they are not powerful enough to influence the status quo.

The point here is that human labor cannot be priced like a commodity. Labor is something completely different, and it needs to be extricated from the economic process. The only way to do that is to see the economy as an independent member of the social body, separate and distinct from the legal, governmental, or political body. Here is an example to clarify what I mean. Economic activity is limited by natural resources. Although our technology may allow us to exploit the land and so on, we cannot do whatever we want with total disregard for natural limits. Just imagine a group of large landowners—capitalists in their own right—"deciding" that to maintain current returns, there will have to be one hundred days of rain each summer, interspersed with so and so many days of sunshine. Of course that would be absolute nonsense, but it does point out that we cannot decide how natural forces will affect this year's grain crop; nor can we alter the economy's base of natural resources in any other way. We must submit to the forces of nature; they exist alongside and independent of the economy.

Similarly, the economy must be limited by the sphere of rights. Natural forces do not depend on economic cycles in the marketplace, and human labor should be similarly independent. Human labor must be recognized as separate and independent from the economy, just as if it were a force of nature. If it is transferred to the sphere of rights, where it belongs, true equality among individuals will develop. Real civil rights can develop only when the true character of human labor is acknowledged. The extent, type, and time of work will be determined before workers enter the economic process. They will then relate as free individuals to their supervisors who will be cultural-spiritual co-workers rather than capitalists, as we will see shortly.

No matter how favorably we view labor contracts, so long as they establish wage relationships, workers will not be satisfied. A humanly worthy existence for all will result only when contractual agreements govern the joint output of supervisors and workers but not labor

itself. Then the worker-supervisor relationship will be one of voluntary partnership. This is what workers basically hope to accomplish,
even though they may not yet be able to articulate it clearly. For the
working class, the actual economic issue (and their actual economic
demand) is to extricate labor from the circulation of goods in the
economy and to establish it as a right within the second member of
the social body, the legal or political system.

Capital must also assume a new form in the context of the political system, although how private property should be reorganized
remains a puzzle to many. The basic principle seems least difficult to
grasp with regard to spiritual property. In this regard our thinking is
already somewhat socially responsible. We recognize that no matter
how clever or talented individuals may be (and in spite of the fact
that they bring their gifts and talents with them at birth, which is a
different issue) they would not be able to produce socially valuable
innovations—whether practical or cultural—in isolation from society.
Although patent and copyright periods vary from place to place and
individuals are allowed to benefit from their intellectual property, we
recognize at least in principle that, in the cultural domain, individual
benefit ceases a certain number of years after the innovator's death.[†]
Intellectual property eventually enters the public domain; it cannot
be passed down indefinitely to heirs who had nothing to do with its
creation.

History demands similar treatment of capital in the future. Just
try to explain this to people educated in the capitalist system and see
how puzzled they look! Nonetheless, one of the most important challenges of our time is to change how capital is incorporated into social
processes. In the future, it will be important for everyone to develop
individual abilities that allow them to manage the means of production in their particular field of work. And the "means of production"
are actually capital. It is in workers' best interests to have managers who are good intellectual leaders so that labor is put to the best
possible use. We must understand that in this situation, the capitalist
becomes an unnecessary fifth wheel. In the future, capital will still
have to be raised to fund the means of production for any branch
of the economy or any cultural purpose. As I described in my book

*Toward Social Renewal*, however, once the individual abilities of the person or groups who raised the capital no longer justify retaining the means of production as personal property, these means of production must be passed to others—not to heirs, but to completely different people, to those best able to manage the means of production for the public good.

In the future, the means of production—that is, capital—will circulate freely in the social body just as blood circulates in the healthy human body. Blood must flow throughout the entire body and cannot be allowed to stagnate anywhere. Similarly, capital will not be allowed to accumulate in the form of private property. When it has served its purpose in one place, it must pass to those who will manage it best. It will thus be relieved of a function that has caused grave social damage.

Clever capitalists quite rightly say that all economic activity involves sacrificing current assets for the sake of future assets. True enough, but if the economy of the past sows the seeds of the economy of the future and ensures its survival, capital needs to share in the properties of goods in general. Again, such statements about future challenges are met with bewilderment. Real goods are consumed, used up. As they are used up, they go the way of living things. In our economy as it has been managed so far, capital has been exempt from this fate of other goods in the economic process. Long ago, Aristotle said that capital should not produce offspring.[†] At present, however, it is producing offspring that grow big and multiply. We can calculate how many years it takes for a capital investment to double if left to its own devices. Capital, however, should actually serve only as a placeholder for other goods, and all other goods eventually either wear out or become unusable if they are not consumed in a timely manner. Monetary investment must become subject to the fate of all other goods. Our current economy expects capital investment to double over a period of time. In a healthy economy, however, invested funds would vanish over that same time period, simply ceasing to exist. Today people are horrified by the suggestion that their monetary investment will not double in fifteen years but will simply vanish because it is consumed or depreciated along with the goods it is used to purchase. Of course certain types of savings could be exempt from this rule.

Today, therefore, we face major economic changes, not just minor adjustments. If we do not summon the courage to trust these changes, the social order—or rather, social disorder or chaos—will overwhelm us. People today have no idea that they are dancing on a volcano. They find it easier to persist in old habits, but our time actually demands not only institutional changes but also re-learning our very ways of thinking.

When labor and capital are extricated from the economy—that is, when capital flows back to the public and labor is given back to free individuals as their right—the only remaining economic processes are the production, circulation, and consumption of goods. The economy then deals only with the values of goods. In the independent economic member of the healthy social body, we will not produce simply in order to go on producing; we will produce in order to consume. Consumers, producers, and professionals will form cooperatives and associations; corporate entities that will serve functions now left to chance in the marketplace. Today, production is governed by supply and demand, which are totally inaccessible to human thinking and human judgment. In the future, these new corporate bodies will decide which factors in commerce will determine price structures—that is, the value of goods. This is the only way that each individual's production will be exactly comparable in value to everything he or she needs until the next round of production. Economic activity will become equitable; the prices of certain goods will not be out of proportion to the prices of other types of goods. Today, when wages are still embedded in the economic process and production workers are not the independent partners of the intellectual workers who are their managers, the workers are always forced to fight for higher wages. But if higher wages close one hole, they open another: groceries become more expensive, and so on. This can happen only in an economy polluted with capital and wage relationships. By contrast, in an economy in which associations or cooperatives determine the value of goods on a rational basis rather than on the basis of supply and demand (which are subject to chance,) every individual will be afforded a humanly worthy existence. Such an economy is truly what the working class is demanding.

This demand is clearer in certain specific areas—for example, in the case of works councils [joint employee-management committees with specific legal powers and responsibilities], which have been so mangled by recent legislation. If the works councils are to become what the working class is demanding, they cannot be set up to serve the state, as intellectual institutions were in the past. Their independent, socially responsible activity must be allowed to thrive in the context of the economy. For this to happen, however, the economy itself must be independent and self-governing. In addition to factory works councils, we will need transportation councils and other councils that develop as needed on the basis of purely economic activity and establish their own bylaws based on economic experience.

I know that a great many people today say that we lack the economic literacy needed to implement such changes. That, however, is how people talk about ideals when they prefer to avoid acting on real possibilities. When we realize that practical knowledge is infinitely more valuable than any knowledge imposed from above, we will recognize the need for works councils not only in individual factories but also as liaisons among very different businesses. They will need to join together in larger associations. As long as their foundations are purely economic, they will not exist simply for decoration but will become the actual human factor in shaping the economy. That is what must happen.

What I have dubbed the threefolding of the social organism is not the product of specious reasoning or murky theorizing. It is based on direct observation of what life demands of us now and will demand in the future. Our present culture provides no real basis for focusing on what reality demands, and as a result very few people are able to do so, which is a real shame. Today people malign truly practical ideas as "ideology" or "utopian." What are the underlying reasons for this negativity? Some say we must socialize the means of production. So do I. But I also say that we need not only goals but also ways of achieving them and the courage to do so. People often tell me that what I say is hard to understand. Admittedly, looking at real life instead of judging it on the basis of subjective demands requires more effort than we are accustomed to applying. It is imperative, however, that we summon the inner courage to think radically about certain things. That is what our time demands of any conscious individual.

I must say that in the past four or five years, I have met people who understood things I did not. They arrived from certain places claiming to understand things they kept in nice frames so they could look at them all the time—things that came from central headquarters and the like. They understood, however, because they were ordered to understand. The understanding that comes from inner courage, however, can never be commanded. Now the time has come when people must no longer permit themselves to be commanded to understand. Instead, we must learn to base our assessment of what is needed on our life experience and in an unbiased way, before it is too late.

In general, I am reluctant to recount personal incidents, but life today is dominated by personal events, and individual experiences can be both strange and representative. In April of 1914, I was obliged to comment on the sociopolitical situation in Europe at a small gathering in Vienna.[†] (Note the time and place; as you know, the catastrophic World War started in Austria.) I said something to this effect: Anyone who looks at the social conditions that have gradually developed must feel great concern for our civilization, because our society has developed a cancer that will soon reach the crisis stage. And in fact the World War broke out a short time later.

At that time I had to point out that international capitalism was driving us into a crisis. Like anyone else making such statements, I was denounced as an impractical idealist or a utopian ideologist, of course. At that time, "practical people" were speaking very differently about the world situation, with no mention of the prospect of a social cancer. Consider, for example, what the German Foreign Minister[†] said to the enlightened members of the German *Reichstag*—we must assume they were enlightened, since they were appointed to their posts—in the spring of 1914. He said: We are heading for peaceful times. We have seen gratifying progress toward a general relaxation of tension. We have a very positive relationship with Russia, and the Cabinet in Petersburg is not listening to the press-hounds. Promising negotiations with England are likely to conclude soon, to the benefit of world peace. Relations between the two governments are continuing to deepen.

These were the words of a "practical" individual who was not derided as an idealist. The "general relaxation of tension" progressed so well that it soon resulted in the crisis we all suffered through. Under the circumstances, it was not entirely comfortable to hear speakers at the recent League of Nations conference† reiterating old, habitual thinking on all sorts of subjects. They failed to say anything relevant about the modern social movement, which is the only thing capable of founding a true league of nations.

These old, habitual ways of thinking often lead to very strange answers coming from very intelligent people. (I certainly don't want to underestimate people's intelligence.) In Bern, one such intelligent gentleman recently told me that he could not imagine that three-folding would accomplish much, since ultimately it all has to come together in a unity; civil rights cannot be limited to the political sphere, and so on.

But my point is that the sphere of rights must develop on its own terms if we are to have "rights" in the economy and in cultural affairs. People say that I am attempting to chop the body social into pieces, but that is not what I am talking about! The point is to give the social organism three strong legs to stand on: a healthy rights sphere, a healthy economy, and healthy cultural institutions. When these exist, the overriding unity will develop of its own accord, and it will be the centralized state we idolize but have to abandon if we want socialism.

For more than a century, people have talked about equality, liberty, and fraternity as the three great social ideals or impulses for human-kind. The highly intelligent people of the nineteenth century, who proved that these ideals could not possibly be achieved had been hypnotized by the idea of the centralized state, and therefore saw these ideals as contradictory. But now it is time to implement these ideals and to take up these three social impulses, which can only be done in the context of the threefold social organism. In a self-determining domain of cultural and intellectual affairs, individual capacities must develop on the basis of *freedom*. In the sphere of rights, which includes employer-employee relationships, the prevailing principle must be the inherent *equality* of all human individuals. And the economy must be governed by the true *sister-and-brotherliness* that can flourish only in cooperative associations, whether of consumers or producers.

Liberty, equality, and fraternity will each be able to prevail in one of the members of the threefold body social. Liberty will thrive in cultural and intellectual affairs, equality in a democratic sphere of rights, and fraternity in economic activity.

Today I have been able to present only a few of the most important perspectives on what we must consider in these serious times if we truly want to escape from chaos and confusion instead of falling deeper into them. Rather than thinking only of small changes, we must summon the courage to admit that a day of great reckoning is upon us. Alert minds see what is coming and realize that we do not have much time to debate what to do. Therefore, let us set out on the path that presents itself to us today: the path to a threefold social order that lies before us. Is this a path of impractical idealism? It seems so only to those who prefer to perpetuate the "practicality" that brought us the catastrophe of a World War.

To heal the body social, we must fundamentally abandon any superstitious idolization of so-called practicality that is nothing more than brute human egotism. We must subscribe to an idealism that is not one-sided but based on real, practical life experience. If we are seriously concerned about our time, we must inquire about ways of healing the grievous injuries that are being inflicted on our society. We can only hope that more and more people will ask this question and find this path before it is too late. It could indeed be too late very soon.

### Concluding Remarks

After a discussion largely dominated by party and union functionaries, Rudolf Steiner rose to speak again:

I am afraid the discussion would have been more fruitful if the speakers had actually gone into the issues I raised. Since that did not happen, I will only be able to draw your attention to a few individual points in the time remaining.

Several speakers said that I did not present anything new. However, I am very familiar with the development of the socialist movement, and what I presented today is based on an actual experience of how the recent international crisis reorganized our society. Anyone who claims that what I said is essentially nothing new needs to be made aware that this claim is fundamentally untrue. The reality of the situation is quite different. The speakers failed to hear the new element in what I presented. They heard only a few obvious and well-deserved criticisms of the existing social order, slogans they have been accustomed to hearing for many years. That is all they heard. They heard absolutely nothing of everything in between, nothing of what I said about the threefolding of the body social or the real socialization it could achieve. Presumably, they failed to mention any of this in their contributions to the discussion because they did not hear it. I understand that. I also understand, however, that this state of affairs cannot lead to a fruitful discussion.

For example, one speaker, who seemed not to have lived through the last five or six years, expounded on the same old theories that had been dealt with so many times before this catastrophe began. He conscientiously restated all the theories of surplus value† and so on, which are certainly quite true, but have already been presented countless times before. The only thing he forgot to consider is that we are now living in quite different times. He forgot, for example, what a highly respected Socialist leader said a few months before the German capitulation: namely, that when this catastrophic World War is over, the German government will have to relate very differently to the working class and involve it in all government actions and legislation. Socialists also said that the Socialist parties would have to be taken into account.

Well, that has not happened. The wielders of power sank into the abyss, and your parties watched it happen. These parties now face a completely different international situation, one that requires us to learn to listen to the most urgent current needs. We must not simply ignore new ideas or choose to hear only the voices of long-standing parties within the socialist movement. If we do, we are in grave danger—a danger that was actually always present in the old international order, which paved the way for reactionaries. How? By dismissing any effort to perceive the reality of the situation and base actions on this reality. Instead, actions were derived from mere ideologies and philosophies having nothing to do with reality. The worst thing that could happen now would be for the Socialist Party to succumb to some sort of reactionary paralysis that would prevent it from actively dealing with the facts, which speak so loudly for themselves.

That is where we stand today. After making the acquaintance of a number of Marxists, Karl Marx himself said: As for myself, I am no Marxist.[†] (Real innovators often have similar experiences.) Marx always showed that he was able to learn from events—in particular, the events of 1870/71[†]—and to adapt to changing times. Today, no doubt, he would admit the possibility that threefolding the body social represents a solution to the social and class problem. Whenever innovators suggest new ways of thinking and acting that require real courage, people say they offer goals but no way of achieving them. Has anyone else introduced the idea of a self-liquidating government? That is truly an unusual idea. Old governments and even the socialist government have no intentions beyond being conscientious extensions of what government used to be. What we need, however, is for government to retain the initiative only in the center—that is, to retain oversight of security services, public hygiene, and the like, while leaving the economy and the domain of cultural affairs to manage themselves.

This is not a theory and not a philosophy. It is an indication of what needs to be done, and the first step in implementing it is to understand that it is necessary. In turn, that understanding requires a willingness to relinquish old habits, and to stop hearing only what we want to hear while ignoring everything unfamiliar.

When speakers get entangled in practical contradictions without noticing it, they demonstrate the impossibility of finding practical ways forward. One speaker, having said first that real political power rests on economic underpinnings, then went on to say (after a number of other remarks, so the juxtaposition was not obvious) that we must seize political power in order to seize economic power. On the one hand, therefore, he is saying that whoever has economic power also has political power. But a few sentences later he says that we must have political power first, and then we will also have economic power. It is impossible to develop practical approaches with people who talk like that. The ability to think clearly, without confused trains of thought, is a prerequisite to any truly practical approach.

We will get no further by clinging to objections such as: Given people's predisposition to comfort and convenience, they will have to be *forced* to send their children to comprehensive schools. That was the reasoning of the former wielders of power. The members of government were truly no more intelligent than their constituents, but they were always convinced that people would do nothing voluntarily and would have to be forced to act.

It is strange to see this sort of reasoning now appearing among socialists, when the reality of the situation demands receptivity to actual needs rather than clinging to entrenched theories and the like. Anyone who says, "We must seize power!" is speaking in vague, theoretical terms. Seizing power without knowing what to do with it results in no progress at all. Go ahead and seize power. Power is for the birds if you have no inkling of what to do once you have it. *Before* coming to power, it is essential to be quite clear about what you intend to use it for.

The revolution of November 9 is over;[†] whether successfully or not is a question of perspective. The international community sees the revolution as bogus because those who seized power do not know what to do next, other than issue calls for unity in accordance with old party platforms. But there is only one way of inspiring unity, namely, to see where the actual damage lies. This is how the threefolding impulse is trying to bring about unity. Objectively speaking, it is simply a slander to say that a new party or a new sect should be founded. That is nonsense. Even if the resolution was passed by numerous assemblies, I am quite certain that it would never be implemented, because doing so would soon unseat those presently in power. There is no reason to fear any threat to unity. But there is one way of effectively destroying unity—just insist on your own principles. Say, "If you do not agree with me, there is no unity." That is what many people today really mean when they preach unity.

As I said before, I regret not being able to go into detail because not one of the speakers who contributed to the discussion really touched on anything I actually presented in my lecture. In the end, they even accused me of philosophizing. These speakers would starve as philosophers, and it is highly debatable whether the last speaker's philosophizing would help us discover anything that might really be helpful in the current situation.

The impulse of threefolding society was first presented in the context of foreign policy during the recent catastrophic war, when I believed the time was right.† That was long before the monstrosity of the peace treaty of Brest-Litovsk.† At that time, on the basis of this threefolding impulse, it seemed right to me to seek some kind of equitable balance with the East, rather than what actually happened. No one understood this, and the well-known consequences of the Brest-Litovsk accord followed. Today it is essential to find people who will act differently than those to whom I initially presented the threefolding idea.

A brochure about responsibility for the war, which will appear in the next few days, will tell the world about how the great crisis broke out and about what was actually going on in Germany in late July and early August of 1914.† It will also show that people did not think for themselves, but were content to let the authorities think for them. This apathy, far from producing a rational foreign policy, led to the nadir of German foreign policy on July 26.† The world needs to be aware of events within Germany in July and August of 1914, which are soon to be brought to light through the memoirs of the individual most involved in those events. We will see what opportunities we missed because the authorities persisted in their usual ways of thinking while everyone else basically allowed themselves to be told what to believe.

But enough about this; we've heard it often before. The war-profiteers were followed by revolution-profiteers; and the warmongers were followed by the revolution-monger; and in both cases their relationship to the profiteers was roughly the same. It is time to move beyond inciting violence and upheaval. We must also move beyond accepting the political leadership of any authorities whatsoever, whether socialists or others. We must become capable of judging for ourselves, but this will not happen if we dismiss all proposals based on the actual requirements of our time.

I will not go into the contributions that distorted and misrepresented the spirit in which my observations were intended. It is objectively inaccurate and derogatory to claim that I attempt to bridge differences with goodwill. I did not talk about bridging differences with goodwill. I talked about organizational changes that need to happen. Making our cultural, economic, and political affairs and their institutions independent of each other has nothing to do with goodwill, but everything to do with objective descriptions of what needs to be done.

I fully agree with anyone who says that we must first have power, but I am not at all clear that wielders of power will know what to do with it. If we simply intend to barge ahead, leaving the unenlightened masses behind, we will find ourselves in much worse circumstances than before.

In contrast to the philosophizing of others, you may feel terribly practical if you say, "The French are completely impoverished and can't give us any bread; England has also been broken by the war and can't give us any bread; America is too expensive for us, but we can get bread from Russia!" Well, in spite of reports to the contrary, it is safe to assume for the moment that the English have much more bread than the Russians. Expecting bread from the Russians has no basis in fact.

The essential point now is to grasp the reality of our situation and to acknowledge that we need new ways of thinking. Our old intellectual institutions were incapable of creating an equitable society. For that we need a new spiritual life, which can be accomplished only by freeing cultural and intellectual/spiritual affairs from political constraints. Similarly, labor needs to be extricated from economic conflicts and protected by an independent constitutional state. We also need equitable pricing, which can happen only in the context of self-regulating economic activity. These are all things we can actually work toward, not mere revolutionary phrases. If we have the courage to introduce them, they will truly change the world. I believe this will become apparent if you apply enough thought to the threefolding of the society. These changes could be introduced in a relatively short time. Once a healthy threefold organism exists, it will revolutionize our circumstances. If it is adopted internationally, we will no longer need to trumpet world revolution, because the revolution will happen as a matter of course. Demanding revolution will not make it happen. It will happen only if we identify seminal ideas that will grow and bear fruit for all.

We do not need to waste much time talking about this, but we do need to understand what must happen. Threefolding society has nothing to do with ideologies, utopias, or philosophies. It is an action plan, a working plan, not a description of some future state. Every house needs a working plan or a blueprint, and so does the reorganization of society. This reorganization will not be implemented by anyone who holds back, whether socialists or others, but only by those who really intend to move forward. I am afraid those of you who heard only "old ideas" and "nothing new" here today would lead us into chaos, not out of it.

For once, let us be seriously receptive to ideas that are unaccustomed and new; ideas that out of complacent habits of thought, we are inclined to ignore completely, editing out all but our own pet phrases. We need to change our thinking. Before it is too late, humankind must appeal to new thinking habits, new mindsets, and new schools of thought. And once again, I tell you, if we do not find the inner courage to do this, it could soon be too late.

# 2

## Insight into the Supersensible Human Being and the Task of Our Time

ULM, JULY 22, 1919

IT is natural to ask about the causes of the hardship and misery all around us at present, but we usually look for these causes in outer circumstances, turning first to the painful experiences of the last four or five years. We may come to realize that this crisis developed gradually, over decades or even centuries in the course of humanity's modern development. The war broke out like a thunderstorm that had gathered strength unnoticed throughout a long, sultry day. But even if we look to the past for the sources of our current situation, we tend to consider outer circumstances and outer solutions—the outer measures and institutions in the hope that they might lead us out of chaos and confusion.

To a great extent, of course, this view is correct, as I attempted to demonstrate when I lectured here on social and class questions several weeks ago. A different view of these issues is also possible, however. That view requires us to become aware of a significant mental phenomenon of our times. We are right to strive for more socially equitable conditions than have been our lot for the last three to four centuries, but we do so out of a very strange mentality. Essentially, modern human souls are full of antisocial drives and instincts that make mutual understanding almost impossible. Life as we know it is the product of centuries of antisocial attitudes and behaviors, and as we strive for greater social equity, we are still acting out of a fundamentally antisocial frame of mind! Viewing the issue from this perspective, we discover that our modern antisocial drives are related to the fact that we have lost the way to the inmost core of the essential being we each intuit within ourselves, whether more or less clearly or only dimly and instinctively. We have lost the way to the supersensible human being. As strange as it may sound, we are no longer conscious of the longings of our inmost souls, which are thirsting for insight into our supersensible nature. In modern times, it is difficult to satisfy this thirst, and the difficulties—although we hate to admit it—account for many of the outer expressions of confusion and chaos we encounter.

Tonight, I will tell you about a possible solution to this problem that differs from many other approaches. Because I approach it from the perspective of anthroposophical spiritual science, I cannot resolve this problem as easily and comfortably as most people today would prefer. When learning about the mountains of the Moon or the moons of Jupiter, for example, and the physical instruments and techniques needed to investigate them, people admit that this knowledge may be complicated and difficult to acquire. They accept that the process may not be easy. When it comes to learning about the supersensible world or the spiritual aspect of human existence, however, people are not so ready to accept difficulties. The way I will speak to you tonight, for example, is "too difficult" for most people to follow. They prefer childish faith to a scientific approach to supersensible worlds. When dealing with our souls' highest aspirations, it is easier to resort to childish faith in the Bible or an established creed and to reject the less comfortable path.

What people fail to recognize today, however, is that to want spiritual development to be easy and comfortable, and to find it difficult to escape from our antisocial drives are intimately related phenomena. We have long been told—and have long believed—that simple, childish confessions of faith can lead to supersensible worlds. If we could come to recognize the connection between this assertion and the antisocial drives we are expressing today, we would change our minds about this "comfortable" path to supersensible worlds.

It is not out of spiritual eccentricity, but out of a real sense of responsibility toward the needs and challenges facing modern humanity, that spiritual science offers modern individuals another way. Real inner self-knowledge shows us that we can no longer be content with the old methods of spiritual development. Many human souls long to find new paths to the spirit, and anthroposophically-oriented spiritual science attempts to satisfy these longings.

Today, as I said, people wonder—whether more or less consciously or more or less unconsciously—about the body-soul connection. (That is, they wonder about it if they are not so worn out by doubts about the human soul that they deny its existence entirely.) But what do we really know about the soul and the body today? We observe the body by using our senses and the same reasoning we apply to outer, physical things. Then, for aspects not directly accessible to our senses and rational thinking, we turn to the natural sciences to learn more about the physical body's intrinsic laws and essential nature. In contrast to outer knowledge of the body, we have inner perceptions of our thoughts, feelings, and intentions, which we associate not only with certain inner desires, wishes, and hopes, but also with the belief that this inner aspect of ourselves has more lasting significance for the world than does the life of the physical body. At this point, however, a question arises that gives birth to grave doubts: How do the thinking, feeling, and willing that I perceive within myself relate to the physical body, which I and others perceive outwardly and which science attempts to explain?

Today we count on having everything explained with due scientific authority, but when we are unable to explain the body-soul connection for ourselves, we discover that there is little to be gained by addressing this question to scientists. We encounter all sorts of hypotheses and assumptions but virtually nothing with the ring of truth to it, and we are generally left with no more certainty than we could provide for ourselves. Finding a convincing explanation is one of the self-imposed tasks of anthroposophically-oriented spiritual science.

But the routes to a scientific understanding of outer phenomena are not the same as the routes to authentic spiritual science. There is usually not much excitement in modern scientific research. When scientists explain what it is like to investigate external natural phenomena in clinics or laboratories, they generally describe going about their work with a certain degree of equanimity. You will hear a very different story from researchers who describe aspects of the route to an understanding of the essential nature of the supersensible human being. When they talk about their experiences, they inevitably mention inner struggles, the need to overcome oneself, and repeated instances of standing at the edge of the abyss of doubt. They will tell you many stories about all they had to overcome and undergo to achieve an understanding of the actual supersensible core of the human constitution.

Doubts about the body-soul connection are among the experiences needed to acquire the intellectual modesty required for perception of this sort. Most people today approach such questions with intellectual arrogance, but we gradually become aware of the need for intellectual modesty if we make a real effort to apply ordinary thinking and other mental powers to the question of the essential character of the human soul and body. We find that our ordinary human thinking and perception are inadequate to the task. The inner effort, however, makes us feel somewhat like five-year-olds holding a volume of lyric poetry. Before five-year-olds can do anything with a book like that (or at least anything pertinent to its essential character), they need help to develop their faculties. We must realize that our ordinary powers of thinking and perception are similarly inadequate for understanding the essential nature of the world and of our own existence.

Developing an inner attitude of intellectual modesty and realizing the inadequacy of our ordinary thinking are the first steps on the path to understanding the supersensible worlds. When we speak about these worlds, both the content and the manner of our speaking are necessarily different from when we talk about the ordinary world of sensory perception. This means, however, that we must take in hand the faculties of thinking and understanding that we apply to ordinary daily life and ordinary science. This is something we can only do for ourselves. Other people help children to develop their faculties through education and upbringing, but we must take our own inner soul faculties in hand and develop them further—especially our thinking, at least initially. My book *How to Know Higher Worlds* provides detailed and systematic descriptions of how to go about this. But tonight, due to the short time available to us, I will be able to present only the most basic aspects.

There is one thing we must understand as a prerequisite to self-development of this sort. When we seek explanations of outer, physical human nature, we turn to scientists. Please note that it is not my intention to belittle the natural sciences. Spiritual researchers see natural science as completely justified and acknowledge its recent great triumphs as fully as natural scientists themselves do. The better the spiritual researcher, the more he or she appreciates the value and significance of the natural sciences. We must realize, however, that our questions to natural science bump into inherent limits of knowledge. You all know that conscientious scientists acknowledge such limits. The concepts and terms used to answer our questions about objects, force, matter, etc., have changed over time, but scientists have always acknowledged the existence of certain limits that human cognition supposedly cannot transcend. In their own fields, natural scientists are right to observe these limits. Clearly these limits cannot apply to spiritual science, but equally important is that spiritual researchers must not attempt to transcend them through mere speculation or fantasizing of any sort.

As they approach subjects beyond the pale of natural science, spiritual researchers experience formidable internal struggles. The battle to overcome natural scientific limits leads to a first great insight, which proves fundamentally important to understanding the supersensible nature of the human being. By struggling with the limits of natural understanding, spiritual researchers realize that our human constitution is uniquely adapted to life. As experience leads them to ask what prevents natural science from seeing into the essential character of the natural world, they discover a strange and shattering fact: If nature were fully transparent, with no limits, we human beings could not possess a certain faculty that we need for our life together between birth and death—namely, the faculty of love! All love between individuals, the brotherly and sisterly love that warms our souls in social encounters with others, would be impossible if nature imposed no limits on our ordinary understanding.

This is a truth that cannot be proved logically, just as the existence or non-existence of whales cannot be proved logically. We believe whales exist because we see them. Similarly, we cannot "prove" that love would not exist if our natural understanding knew no limits. This truth, however, is a matter of direct experience for anyone who achieves a certain degree of spiritual cognition and "sees" the secrets that our human existence conceals. One such secret is that we gain the capacity for love by losing our initially unlimited natural understanding and vice versa.

This insight, however, also reveals what we must overcome in order to gain access to the spiritual world that houses the inmost core of our being. This is one of the fundamental principles of all paths of spiritual development in general: If we are not to lose love as we transform our thinking into something more than the ordinary, we must increase our capacity for love—our loving devotion to all of the world's beings—above and beyond the love we bestow in ordinary life between birth and death. Preparation for the path of spiritual knowledge includes becoming much more capable of love than we need to be in our ordinary interactions with each other. In fact, we gradually become aware that as long as we occupy physical bodies, love is the only way our undivided human nature can learn about the world. Love is the only research method available to us.

To gain access to the spiritual world, our thinking must develop beyond the level it would naturally achieve. We can reach this higher level by systematically disciplining ourselves to perform specific mental activities that we would perform only perfunctorily or coincidentally in ordinary life. Tonight I can present only a few details about the exercises that are described at length in *How to Know Higher Worlds*, but I will at least be able to give you some idea of the basis for the higher development of human thinking.

When we perceive an outer stimulus of any sort, we pay attention to it. When we hear a sound, we develop an interest in what is happening where the sound came from. Typically, the mental activities of *interest* and *attentiveness* are stimulated from outside. The path to spiritual perception involves voluntary and deliberate application of energy, interest, attentiveness, etc.— as in meditation, for example, where we may focus our consciousness on a single mental image for a long time. In everyday life, we would soon lose interest in that image and stop paying attention to it. But suppose we deliberately dwell on it for a period of time, reinforcing our interest or attentiveness from within whenever it slackens. Doing this exercise repeatedly strengthens our thinking and transforms it. Just as any manual work takes effort, this new thinking is full of inner activity that takes effort on our part, and it is related to our ordinary thinking in the same way that our ordinary adult thinking relates to that of a five-year-old confronted with lyric poetry, for example.

Having achieved this new thinking, we realize that the inner effort it requires is as tiring to the body as years of hard physical labor. When we recognize that the mental effort of working on ourselves is as strenuous as chopping wood, for example, we have grasped living, inward thinking. By contrast, our ordinary thinking simply follows along with outer phenomena and events. Reflect for a moment on how you think in everyday life: You go about your work, and your thinking runs alongside in a dreamy sort of way. If you challenge your thinking by reading a difficult book, however, you soon discover that inwardly active thinking is as tiring as any other activity. If we carry this process ever further, we will notice that our thinking changes into a type of thinking we never dreamed of before. Our ordinary thinking is a mere reflection of this new thinking, which is inwardly alive and does not depend on either the brain or the body for its instrument. If we follow the path outlined in *How to Know Higher Worlds*, it will become evident—as grotesque, paradoxical, or crazy as this may sound today—that the spiritual essence we grasp through inward, active thinking is completely independent of the instrument of the brain. I am not talking about any new development, because this spiritual essence does not "develop." We simply become aware of its presence. We perceive the supersensible essence of the human being.

At this point, we also recognize the grave error of both ordinary science and the views on thinking popular in our materialistic age. Science tells us that the brain is the instrument of thinking, but this is just as wrong as imagining that tire tracks and footprints on a muddy dirt road develop from below as the result of underground forces.

Clearly, that interpretation is ridiculous. Nothing in the makeup of the soil tells us anything about how these marks appeared, because they were imprinted from above by people and cars passing by. When we become familiar with body-free thinking, we recognize that ordinary science makes a similar mistake. The nerves and convolutions of the brain do not house forces that produce consciousness. They are merely imprints of a mental activity that is independent of the body. Mental activity leaves physical traces on the brain, but the body does not produce these traces; they are imprinted on it by an active essence.

This active essence, however, is not always easy to grasp. It takes a considerable presence of mind to catch even a brief glimpse of body-free human thinking. Spirit flares up in our ordinary perception and fades away with the speed of lightning. As you can read in *How to Know Higher Worlds*, cultivating what we call "presence of mind"— the ability to assess situations and respond to them rapidly—is good preparation to become aware of the spirit. By cultivating the faculty of presence of mind, we prepare ourselves to see what appears out of the spiritual, supersensible world. Normally, we lack the presence of mind to look at such flashes of spirit before they disappear. But when we learn to catch these glimpses of the spiritual world—that is, when our developed thinking recognizes the spirit-dwelling aspect of the human being—we see beyond ordinary, everyday human life and acquire a completely different perspective.

One unique characteristic of spiritual perceptions is that they cannot be remembered in the ordinary sense of the word. When seers talk about the spiritual world, they cannot simply recall what they once saw, but must repeatedly recreate the circumstances that allow them to see it. But if spiritual perception is as fleeting and rapidly forgotten as a dream, it nonetheless contains a memory of a very significant sort.

At this point, it is important to inject a comment that will necessarily sound very strange to people today. Centuries ago, it must have sounded equally strange when people first heard that what appear to be mere points of light in the night sky are actually countless worlds distributed throughout space. That certainly must have been difficult to believe at first, but people got used to the idea, and now we accept it as a matter of course. Similarly, the experiences that spiritual researchers achieve by developing their thinking may sound strange now, but in a couple of centuries they will be accepted as common knowledge. One of the tasks of our time is to develop people's understanding for this expansion of human cognition and perception.

When we are applying inwardly alive, body-free thinking, ordinary memory is inaccessible to us. Instead, we look back on the life of spirit and soul that we lived in a purely spiritual world before descending into the sense-perceptible world and uniting with physical human bodies through conception and birth. Our view expands beyond bodily life to reveal the life in the spiritual world from which we descended to enter physical existence.

This insight also gives a completely new meaning to all of our human interactions. When we encounter people socially, we develop sympathy for some more quickly than for others. We develop a great variety of connections to other people during this life between birth and death. When we acquire a spiritual researcher's insight into life, we discover that anything that attracts us to one person or more or less alienates us from another—in short, any interpersonal connection we develop—is the consequence of experiences with that other soul in a different world, before we descended into our current physical existence. Everything we experience in the physical world is revealed as a reflection of experiences in the spiritual world.

I have described a modern way to achieve perception of the spiritual world through mental effort. Many people today may be unable to acknowledge this possibility, but they are simply not keeping pace with the times. When the first railroad was about to be built in Germany, a group of physicians and other experts was convened to deliver an informed opinion on whether or not railroads should be built.[†] These experts advised against building railroads on the grounds that rail travel would be hazardous to health and that only fools would choose to ride the trains. At the very least (if construction proceeded against all better judgment) it would be necessary to erect a tall board fence on either side of the tracks to prevent concussions in people standing close to the passing trains. Today some people believe—

figuratively speaking—that hearing spiritual researchers talk about their insights into the supersensible world will cause concussions; but continued progress will overcome this prejudice, just as we have overcome other prejudices in the past.

Many people who despair of finding inner satisfaction in old religious traditions turn to so-called mysticism, believing that if they sink ever deeper into their own souls, the true inner nature of the human being will bubble up as if from some mystical source. This approach also has limits, which spiritual researchers must learn to recognize. It is important to acknowledge mysticism, just as we acknowledge the natural sciences. But we cannot be constrained by either approach. We must learn that mysticism by itself leads only to illusions about the supersensible makeup of the human being, not to real knowledge. Legitimate spiritual researchers are truly not illusionists. They have no illusions about what should be accepted as reality. Unlike ordinary mystics, they do not begin by attempting to conjure up all sorts of fantastical phenomena from within themselves. Through the struggle to control and direct their own inner activity, they recognize that mystical discoveries are essentially limited to impressions of the period since birth. These impressions may have been received subconsciously rather than being clearly perceived, but they persist in memory nonetheless.

Even natural scientists have made pertinent observations in this regard. The following example from scientific literature is only one out of hundreds and thousands.[†] A scientist is walking past the display window of a bookstore when his glance falls on the title of a book, and he breaks out laughing. There is nothing funny about the title, so he cannot understand his sudden urge to laugh. He closes his eyes, thinking it might be easier to solve this puzzle without the distraction of the outer impression. With eyes closed, he hears something he did not notice before—the sound of a hurdy-gurdy in the distance. As he continues to listen, he identifies the melody as one he once danced to. At that time, he was paying more attention to his dance partner or perhaps to the dance steps, and so the melody made very little impression on him. That slight impression, however, was strong enough to recall later in life when he heard a hurdy-gurdy play the same melody again.

Spiritual researchers, being well aware of such instances and their true character, do not succumb to illusions. They know that mystical talk about experiencing the divine, eternal human being within sometimes has no more significance than a hurdy-gurdy melody. It is simply the recollection of past events that have been altered in subconscious memory. The paths of ordinary mysticism will lead you to nothing more than what you have already perceived. If you aspire to become only a mystic, you may succumb to terrible illusions.

For spiritual researchers, this is another boundary to cross or limitation to transcend. For them, it is a matter of direct experience— although one not "logically" provable—that attempting to achieve spiritual perception by looking inside oneself is neither safe nor effective. If we go this route, we risk losing another mental faculty necessary for ordinary life: namely, memory. Healthy memory depends on the health of all other mental faculties. Disturbances of memory indicate that the "I" itself is disturbed—a terrible mental illness. Just as the limits of natural cognition allow us to *love*, our ability to *remember* is due to the impossibility of discovering the higher nature of the human being through inward-directed vision.

We can, however, take steps to consolidate and strengthen the faculty of memory to a greater extent than occurs naturally. Exercises for this purpose are also described in my book *How to Know Higher Worlds* I mentioned earlier. If you make a practice of reviewing the events of your day each evening, visualizing them very clearly, you safeguard and strengthen the mental faculty of memory to serve purposes above and beyond those of everyday life. The next step would be to take your own "I" consciously in hand by doing exercises that deliberately cultivate new habits. Think for a moment about how you have changed in the last week, month, year, or decade. If you compare your present mental state to that of ten or twenty years ago, the inner growth and development becomes obvious. For the most part, however, we develop unconsciously. Life itself forces us to change.

I have already described how thinking can be developed consciously. Similarly, we can also cultivate our intentions and actions deliberately. We move toward conscious self-discipline by always being aware of what we do badly and of opportunities to learn from life. In ordinary life, we are not aware of the dark workings of our will. If we take our development in hand by observing our own intentions and actions, we will find that our will gradually becomes thought-filled. When observing our own, willing becomes a concrete soul-spiritual experience, the higher will faculty thus developed joins forces with the enhanced thinking that we developed through other exercises. As a result, we gain the ability to perceive an aspect of ourselves that seems so completely independent of any bodily activity that we know we will carry it through death into the spiritual world. By cultivating our thinking, we come to perceive the spiritual life that precedes conception and birth; and by cultivating our will, we become acquainted with the spiritual life we live after death. You see, spiritual science cannot talk about the supersensible human being in any ordinary way. Instead, it must tell us how to gain the experience needed to perceive human life before birth and after death.

Through this approach to the world and to our own essential human nature, we also approach interpersonal matters in a new way. We observe the experiences we share with certain people. We note how circumstances bring us together or separate us, how we relate to others through friendship, and so on. We learn to recognize that all of these connections in the physical, sense-perceptible world will continue to develop after we pass through the portal of death. Life after death becomes a concrete reality when we know that our earthly connections to other people will survive death.

Today these ideas still sound strange—yet one of the tasks of contemporary culture is to come to terms with them. If we succeed in developing the faculties I have described, we will see human history and humankind's development in a whole new light. In the future, what we call "history"—now simply a fable we agree to believe—will have to become something completely different. At the end of my lecture tonight, I will give you an example to illustrate how human beings of the future will have to gain independent access to humankind's historical development.

In our usual view of history, we fail to notice a significant turning point in humanity's development in the middle of the fifteenth century. It is commonly said that nature does not proceed by leaps and bounds—a statement that is almost universally believed, although it is quite false. Nature *always* moves in leaps and bounds. Just consider how a plant develops: leaves appear first, then flowers with their pistils and stamens, and finally the fruit. Similar leaps occur in historical events, and one of them took place in the mid-1400s. We simply fail to notice it because our view of history is so superficial. Seeing into the spirit of historical activity requires an expansion of human perception that can come to grips with outer historical events as readily as it masters events between birth and death. Such perception reveals that the mid-1400s mark the beginning of an age that will last a long time. This age succeeded another one, which had lasted from the eighth century B.C. until the middle of the fifteenth century A.D., spanning two cultures (the exquisitely beautiful Greek culture and the culture of Rome) and the aftermath of both. The mid-1400s marked the beginning of our modern culture.

The inherent difference between Greco-Roman and modern cultures is not yet perceptible to modern human beings. From the eighth century B.C. to the fifteenth century A.D., human capacity for development was quite different from what it is today. Let me clarify this with an example: First, imagine a child in the years before the beginning of the second dentition (around age seven) and the epoch-making changes it ushers in. My book *The Education of the Child*"[†] explains what the details of this event signify to those capable of observing human nature more closely. To put it briefly, there are parallels between physical and psychological development. The next turning point occurs at puberty, around age fourteen. In successive phases, parallels in the development of body and spirit become less apparent, although they persist to some extent until approximately age twenty-seven, when bodily development comes to completion in modern human beings, as has been the case since the mid-1400s.

In Greek and Roman times, however, physical and psychological development continued in parallel until around age thirty-five, although not to the extent evident in the second dentition and puberty. This infinitely significant fact of human historical development, revealed through spiritual research, accounts for the noteworthy harmony of body and soul in ancient Greek culture. Humankind's history reveals that the number of years in which we can emancipate ourselves from our physical, bodily nature has decreased. The result has been a very different relationship of the soul-spiritual aspect of the individual to the world spirit. From the eighth century B.C. to the fifteenth century A.D., the reasoning and emotions of individuals developed on a more instinctive level. The life of this time period was pervaded with instinctive intellectual and emotional activity. Since the mid-1400s, however, individuals have developed more conscious rationality and emotions and have increasingly experienced themselves as independent personalities.

This historical shift also explains why great events in humankind's evolution fall into one or the other of these time periods. The Mystery of Golgotha and the founding of Christianity, the central event that gives meaning to Earth's evolution as a whole, took place during the first third of the age preceding ours, when human beings still remained capable of bodily development into their thirties. In that age of instinctive rational and emotional forces, people instinctively related to this central event in the right way—namely, naïvely rather than consciously. They realized that they were witnessing an event not entirely of human origin. They understood that when the supersensible being of the Christ united with the body of Jesus of Nazareth, a supersensible being intervened in the Earth's development. The physical facts of what happened on Golgotha were only the outer expression of a supersensible event in the context of earthly development.

At that time, this great event was understood instinctively. Meanwhile, since the middle of the fifteenth century, rational and emotional forces that were formerly instinctive have become conscious. This increased consciousness made possible not only the zenith of natural scientific development but also outer industrialization and materialism, which were the inevitable side-effects of the dominance of the independent personality. It is now time to abandon this materialism by seeking access to the spiritual world in the new way I have described here today. Our modern age became materialistic as the consciousness soul developed out of the human soul's older, instinctive manifestation. This shift led to materialism not only in outer life but also in theology. Consider for a moment the extent to which theology and religion have succumbed to materialism. In the age of the consciousness soul, people have become incapable of recognizing the supersensible character of the events on Golgotha and are proud of interpreting them in terms of sense-perceptible reality. Even many theologians are proud of the fact that they no longer see the Christ as a supersensible being, who descended into an earthly human body, but rather as the "simple man from Nazareth"—greater than other human beings, no doubt, but still only human. At least so far, our materialistic age has failed to recognize the Mystery of Golgotha—the Christ's death and resurrection—as the greatest event in the evolution of humanity and the cosmos. Religion itself is becoming materialistic. This process cannot be halted by simple faith, but only by the conscious spirit-cognition of which I spoke today, which will again rise to the understanding that a super-earthly, supersensible being lived in the body of Jesus of Nazareth, thus uniting himself with humanity's further evolution. Anthroposophically-oriented spiritual science is pulling the Mystery of Golgotha back into focus for humanity, but in a way that divests it of the narrow-mindedness of individual denominations and creeds.

As spiritual perception of the supersensible human being continues to develop, it will be able to find a home in every individual on Earth, regardless of race or nationality. Because perception of this sort also leads to the Mystery of Golgotha, human beings everywhere on Earth will learn to understand that event. In our time, it is so easy for people to wax enthusiastic about the utopian League of Nations that developed in the highly abstract thinking of Woodrow Wilson.[†] It is the task of our time to develop a true association of peoples, but this is not how it will come about. It needs a foundation in reality, a foundation that originates in the inmost human soul. The only force that can lead to a true worldwide association of peoples in the future is the soul faculty that leads to perception of the supersensible human being and to acknowledgement of the supersensible character of the Christ event. These impulses transcend nationality, ethnicity, and national boundaries, and will unite all individuals on earth. Christianity must become rooted in human culture in a new way.

I have said all this to show you the inner aspect of what I said in my last lecture here. This aspect is the human mindset that will once again spark truly social impulses. The ability to accept the other natural sciences depends on information accessible only to astronomers, physicians or the like. Accepting spiritual science, however, does not require any faith in authority. You do not need to accept what spiritual researchers tell you on authority, nor do you need to be a spiritual researcher yourself; just as you do not need to be an artist in order to find beauty in a painting. You can accept spiritual science on the authority of your own healthy human reason if you first simply eliminate the prejudices fostered by modern materialism. The seeds of spiritual science lie dormant in the depths of all human souls; access to them does not require faith in authority. If incorporated into our modern culture, trust in the revelations of spiritual science will rebuild that culture and serve as leavening for outer institutions of renewal.

What do we see when we truly attempt to understand the essence of our present time? I would say that we see two possible routes: one leading to the left and one to the right. One would allow us to retain the perspectives provided exclusively by the natural sciences and to apply those same perspectives to societal issues. In other words, this route begins with the belief that we can understand public affairs by using the same store of ideas that we use for understanding the natural world. Karl Marx and Friedrich Engels took this route, just as Lenin and Trotsky are doing so now. People today do not yet realize that the ultimate consequence of this misdirected scientific approach is social chaos or social decline. The horrendous beliefs of Lenin and Trotsky, which are now threatening to destroy any true human culture in Eastern Europe, are based on the belief that the natural scientific approach also applies to societal issues. But what has happened under the influence of the relatively recent convictions of materialistic science? As a consequence of our mechanistic view of nature, our entire intellectual life has become mechanized and no longer rises to a level that permits thinking about the supersensible human being. Simultaneously, human souls are becoming "vegetized"—made plant-like and sleepy. Mechanized spirit and "vegetized" soul set the tone of modern cultural life. And when human souls are not warmed by spirit, and human spirits are not illumined by supersensible cognition, human bodies develop the animalistic qualities now evident in antisocial drives. In Eastern Europe in particular, these animalistic qualities are becoming the executioners of culture; and all attempts at socialization are having the worst possible antisocial consequences. The wildest instincts and drives are masquerading as historic trends and demands. This is the route that leads to the left.

The route to the right is the route that I have described today, the path to perceiving the supersensible human being and the supersensible world. This route sheds supersensible light on human development striving upward toward the truly free spirit.

The purpose of the ideas about free human progress that I attempted to formulate in *The Philosophy of Freedom* was to point to spiritual activity as the basis of our becoming conscious of real inner freedom. Only the spirit that indwells each individual can be truly free. The spirit that pervades only the natural world becomes mechanistic and unfree when it serves as a model for all of our public activity. Souls pervaded only by this spirit are asleep, like plants, unlike souls warmed through by the true, pulsing will to perceive and value the supersensible aspect of human nature. These souls learn to behold the divine archetype in every human being and to feel socially responsible toward all. They learn that all human beings on earth are equal with regard to their inmost souls. On the route leading to the right, *equality* is cultivated by souls warmed through by spirit. When spirit arouses souls from their vegetative state, bodies are ennobled and imbued with an awareness of the supersensible. These bodies do not become animalistic, but develop real love in the broadest sense. When this happens, individuals recognize themselves as supersensible beings, who enter earthly bodies in order to learn to love spirit. They also know that earthly bodies need brotherly-sisterly love, because individuals cannot be fully human so long as humanity is without brotherly-sisterly love.

We see, therefore, that continuing in the old way leads to mechanized spirit, vegetized souls, and animalized bodies. By contrast, spiritual science points to a path leading to true social virtues that are illumined by spirit, warmed with soul, and implemented by ennobled human bodies. Achieving spiritual perception of the supersensible human being leads toward a future housed in a beautiful new edifice based on:

—*Freedom* in intellectual and cultural affairs. Spirit-imbued individuals will be free individuals.

—*Equality* in our spirit-warmed soul activity. Souls receptive to spirit perceive and treat other souls they encounter in life as equals in a great mystery.

—Genuine *brotherly-sisterly love* practiced by bodies ennobled by spirit and soul.

Understanding the real nature of body, soul, and spirit will lead to a human social order based on liberty, equality, and fraternity.

# 3

## Realizing the Ideals of Liberty, Equality, and Fraternity through Social Threefolding

### BERLIN, SEPTEMBER 15, 1919

For modern humanity, the catastrophic World War and its aftermath have undoubtedly put a new face on questions of society and class. Unfortunately, far fewer people have acknowledged this change than we might hope. Nonetheless, it has occurred and will continue to make itself felt with ever-increasing emphasis.

The facts themselves will force members of today's ruling circles to realize that their approach to social problems can no longer be limited to ideas and measures formulated in response to pressing events in individual economic sectors, or to the demands of specific working-class groups. These leading circles or classes will be forced to broaden their approach by focusing their thoughts and actions on the social and class issue as a whole, which is indeed the most important issue facing us at present and in the near future. Not only the leading classes but also the rank-and-file of the working class will need to significantly alter their approach in order to effectively incorporate this new face of the social issue into their thinking, feeling, and willing in ways adapted to the time we live in.

For more than half a century, the working class has been grappling with ideas of socialism and social change. Unless we slept through the past few decades, we all saw the transformations that the social question has undergone in the rank-and-file of the working class. We saw the face it assumed when the horrible catastrophe of the World War broke out. With the provisional end of this catastrophe, the working class (at least in Central and Eastern Europe) found itself in a new situation, no longer simply yoked into a social order driven by the old ruling powers. To a considerable extent, the working class itself was called upon to participate in reshaping social institutions—an unprecedented state of affairs. But then we experienced an extraordinary tragedy: the ideas to which the working class had devoted decades of blood and sweat proved unsustainable when the time came to implement them.

We experienced a great historical contradiction—a conflict, actually—as we realized that the historical facts unfolding around us were poised to become humanity's great instructors. On the one hand, these facts made it clear that the ruling classes of the last three or four centuries had not developed any ideas capable of steering events now unfolding in the economy and other aspects of human society. The people with the power to take real action simply allowed events to unfold on their own. The realities of life had grown too big for us, and the thoughts and ideas of the leading classes proved too narrow to embrace the facts. For a long time, this strange state of affairs was especially evident in the economy, where competition in the so-called "free market" emerged as the only regulating factor, leaving "profit" and the like in the dust. Economic activity was essentially left to chance, and proposals to limit the economy to issues of the production, circulation, and consumption of goods had no impact. A series of crises ensued. It became evident to anyone who chose to be conscious of it that the great empire-states were ultimately infected by the same mindless activity and began to spin out of control. At that point, no one had any thoughts capable of guiding the inexorable course of events.

Today, we really ought to ponder our recent history and consider the possibility that we need a more profound insight into human affairs. Social questions now require a new and different type of understanding. We fail to realize the obvious: our thoughts have fallen short when confronted with the momentum of recent events. In the last three or four centuries, we have blithely assumed that "business as usual" is the "practical" approach, and that anyone capable of a broader overview is either a utopian or an impractical idealist. Let me illustrate this statement with a seemingly personal observation, although the fact that it is personal is not the point. Today, when the destiny of individuals is so closely linked to the general destiny of humankind, only sincere facts observed by individuals adequately illustrate the impulses and driving forces at work in public life.

In the early spring of 1914, just months before the outbreak of the so-called World War, I gave a series of lectures on spiritual-scientific subjects to a small group of people in Vienna.† (I would have been laughed off the stage if I had said the same thing to a larger audience.) In the course of one of these lectures, I was asked to give my views on current social developments. I said that to supersensible perception, events in the public life of the civilized world appear very seriously diseased, as if penetrated by a social carcinoma. I said that this insidious sickness in our economy and our society in general would soon break forth in the form of a terrible catastrophe. That was what I saw beneath the surface of events.

But in the spring of 1914, what did they call people who spoke of impending catastrophe? They called us "impractical idealists"—which was simply a way to avoid calling us idiots. What I felt obliged to say at that time contrasted starkly with what so-called "practical" people were saying. These responsible, self-styled pragmatists were really just creatures of habit, but they belittled anyone who was attempting to understand contemporary history on the basis of ideas of whatever sort. But what were the pragmatists saying at that time? One of them, the foreign minister of a central European country, announced to the illustrious representatives of his nation that admirable progress was being made toward a general relaxation of tension in the political situation, and that we could look forward to a state of peace among the European nations in the near future.† He added that our friendly connections to St. Petersburg were (and would continue to be) the best they had ever been, since the St. Petersburg cabinet was ignoring the press-hounds, thanks to the efforts of the Russian government. Moreover, our negotiations with England, which would soon be concluded, were expected to result in the best possible relationships with that country in the very near future. Now, the man who said this was a "pragmatist" and any predictions to the contrary were "murky theories"!

I could give you countless other examples of pragmatic insightfulness at the beginning of that terrible period of time. The facts speak for themselves. It was actually very instructive to hear these pragmatists talking about peace and then a few months later to see the peace violated to such an extent that the civilized nations then spent several years killing ten to twelve million people, at a conservative estimate, and crippling three times as many. I mention these facts not for sensational effect but simply because they indicate the inadequacy of people's thinking. We will see these events in the right light only when we allow the facts to tell us what we need to do to restore healthy social circumstances. We should not be thinking about minor adjustments. Significant re-learning and significant changes in thinking are required. We face a major day of reckoning: nothing that has grown old, unsound, and rotten can be allowed to carry over into our efforts toward the future.

Such statements about humanity's overarching concerns also apply individually to our political and economic affairs. Wherever we look, people are expressing thoughts that are inadequate for coming to grips with realities. The leading classes have the power to control practical activity, but lack any truly practical ideas and thoughts to put into practice. Confronting these leading classes is the rank-and-file of the working class, rigorously self-educated in Marxist thought for more than half a century. It is relatively easy—sometimes very easy—to objectively disprove the economic thinking of the working class rank-and-file and leadership, but that is not the point. The proletarian theory, the fallout from this intensive schooling in Marxist thought in the hearts and minds of the working class, is a historical reality. But when this theory had an opportunity to prove itself in actual practice when the old order collapsed, it revealed a very understandable shortcoming. Over the last few centuries (especially the nineteenth), the influence of private capital and modern technology had increasingly limited the working class to exclusively economic activity and defined each individual's work very narrowly. Individual routines were essentially all the working class saw of an economy that was constantly expanding its scope. Not surprisingly, the working class experienced the development of the modern economy in terms of its fateful impact on individual bodies and souls, but never acquired an overview of the driving forces at work in this development. The workers' position in the economy prevented them from achieving any objective view of the economy's structure or management. All too understandably, we are now seeing the fruits of this state of affairs: The subconscious, instinctive drives and demands of the working class have given rise to an extensive socialist theory that is essentially very far removed from economic or other social realities, because the working class was rendered incapable of achieving any overview of the actual driving forces behind these realities, and was therefore forced to accept the one-sided view Marxism offered. Over the centuries, certain concepts that are completely justified, yet fail to address the realities of the situation, have become deeply entrenched in the minds of the working class.

Let me give you an example. Just think of the agitation aroused in the working class by its leaders' theoretical views, such as the words, "In the future, production must occur not for its own sake but only to support consumption." This statement is certainly pertinent and even "true" (unlike many contemporary slogans), but it becomes an elusive, empty abstraction if we do not think it through practically; that is, with real insight into economic conditions. What does it mean in actual practice? What are its implications for how we do things? Simply demanding that production be matched to consumption has no effect on actual practice. It simply conjures up an image of how wonderful it would be if our economy were dominated by realistic prospects of consumption instead of by the profit motive. Nothing in this demand suggests *how* the economy would have to be organized to bring about the desired state of affairs. The same could be said about many phrases that have become proletarian party slogans. Although some of these slogans are based on profound truths, they have become abstractions that sound like utopian visions of some indefinite point in the future. If we mean well by the working class, we must realize that in spite of its justified demands, its working theory is far removed from life's realities because workers have been isolated from the full scope of economic activity and secluded in locations where all they ever see is fragments of the larger reality.

This is the conflict I wanted to point out: on the one hand, the ruling classes have the power to influence the actual state of affairs, but no ideas that would allow them to do so. On the other hand, the working class has ideas, but these ideas are highly abstract and remote from the realities of the situation.

Such statements point to the activity of historical forces and impulses that are more fundamentally significant than any events in human history. The true weight of phrases such as "the absence of ideas in leading circles" and "the impracticality of proletarian theory" can be felt only if we sense the mutually destructive impact of these conflicting trends in modern developments. The profound contrast between the thinking, emotions, intentions, and actions of the leading class on the one hand and the longings, desires, and will impulses of the working class on the other has deepened into a veritable abyss. We do not even really understand the full depth of modern proletarian demands. When we hear proletarian theories about surplus value, about the need to match production to consumption, or about the collectivization of private property, we certainly understand the words, but are they meant to elicit logical criticism in response? To a corporate lawyer or the director of a corporation, the logical response is that the sum total of surplus value is so low that if it were shared equally, no one would get anything at all. But what could possibly be more naïve than relating to the theory of surplus value in this way? I do not mean to dispute the gentleman's calculations, but they are not the point. Such attempts at "refuting" proletarian theories are like holding a match under the thermometer if the temperature in the room is not to your liking. Attempts to "correct" the thermometer have no impact on the underlying cause. To take the theories of the modern working class at face value and then refute them is simply naïve, because these theories express much deeper concerns. Like a thermometer that *indicates* but does not *cause* the temperature of a room, proletarian theories are indicators of more profound factors at work in modern class issues. In an era dominated by private capital and technology, we first encounter class issues in economic form—namely, in the demands of a working class whose experience is limited entirely to the economy. As a result, we tend to take these issues at face value and view them as purely economic in character. We fail to see what lies behind proletarian theories about capital, labor, and goods. Working-class people experience all of human life in the economic field, so their perspective on social issues is also entirely economic.

Anyone with the opportunity to achieve a broader view, however, should be able to distinguish three clearly different spheres of life, in which the three essential social issues are revealed. Anyone who has learned to think and feel *with* rather than *about* the working class sees through the key words of socialist theory to what is stirring in the souls of the best of the working class. But what are these key words?

The first, as I have already pointed out, is *surplus value*. Anyone who has associated extensively with working-class people on a personal level must realize how deeply this concept has impacted proletarian hearts and minds. During crucial years in the development of the modern workers' movement, I was working here in Berlin at the Workers' School founded by Wilhelm Liebknecht.† From life experience, therefore, I know more than some union leaders. How can I put this without causing offence? I certainly know more than socialist revolution-mongers. But what does surplus value mean? Workers produce goods. Business owners then sell the finished goods and pay the workers enough so they can stay alive and continue working. The value the workers' labor adds to the raw materials more than covers the costs of production. The rest is "surplus value." What Walther Rathenau,† for example, says about this excess is certainly correct. I do not want to further malign this controversial figure. With regard to the overall class issue, however, he is gravely mistaken. It is certainly true that surplus value, if distributed equally, would not suffice to improve the lot of the rank-and-file. We cannot get to the bottom of the matter through unsubstantiated accounting operations. But is this surplus value really as small as Rathenau's "accurate" calculations indicate? Of course not! If it were, Berlin would have no theaters, universities, prep schools, or any of the other trappings of human culture, all of which are largely supported by so-called surplus value. For us, however, the point is not how surplus value comes to the surface in goods and in the circulation of money. The point is that this catchword expresses the entire relationship of modern cultural life to the rank-and-file, who cannot participate in it directly.

In my years as an instructor of working-class adults, I always attempted to speak to my students in universally human terms and about subjects accessible to all, regardless of class. As a result, I know something about what the character of a universal education would look like and how different it would be from the intellectual and cultural education that has developed over the past three or four centuries under the influence of private capital and the industrial economy. Let me give another personal example that I hope will illustrate a more general principle. When my words resonated with my working-class students, I could tell that they were receptive to the information or perceptions I was attempting to convey. There were other times, however, when our classes had to do the fashionable thing and participate in the "culture" of the leading classes. Taking my working-class students to museums and the like put bourgeois culture on display for them, but it did nothing to bridge the gap between it and their intellectual needs and longings. Honest teachers admitted it; the rest mouthed clichés about educating the masses and so on. We understand art, science, and religion only when they are based on the shared perceptions and emotions of our peer group—not when there is a rift between those who are supposed to enjoy culture and those who actually *can*. We experienced this discrepancy as a profound cultural lie, and it is now time to stop obscuring it with good intentions and see it for what it is. The lie consisted in establishing all kinds of adult education centers to impart "culture" to people who could not find a bridge to it in their own lives. Workers stood on the other side of the chasm, looking across at bourgeois art, conventions, religion, and science but not understanding them, seeing them only as inaccessible luxuries, of interest only to the leading class—and as the fruits of surplus value. For members of the working class, "surplus value" was not just an indicator (like a thermometer), but a culture that excluded them, though their labor produced it.

When we understand not only the theory of surplus value but also its unforeseen impacts in real life, we recognize the first essential component—the cultural face, so to speak—of the all-encompassing issue of social justice. As technology, modern science, and capitalism developed over the last three or four centuries, the emerging culture increasingly reflected only a bourgeois inner life separated by a deep chasm from the life of the working class. The cultural elite neglected the education and culture of the masses. It's enough to make your heart bleed to think about how members of the upper classes gathered to talk about "brotherly" love and all such Christian virtues in rooms heated with coal mined by children as young as nine. In the mid-1800s, these poor children literally never saw daylight on weekdays because they went down into the mines before sunrise and came up only after sundown. Credit for later improvements in these conditions is due to proletarian demands, not to any effort on the part of the upper classes. Today, anyone who talks about this history is accused of rabble-rousing. Not true! The intention is simply to point out that over the last three or four centuries, cultural and intellectual affairs have become increasingly isolated from the real life of ordinary people. It has become quite possible to speak about morality, Christian virtues, religion, brotherly love, loving your neighbor, etc., without taking action or having any effect on real, practical everyday life. This is the key point revealed by the cultural face of the social justice issue.

All of this points to the field of education. Along with other important public aspects of culture, the school system has been absorbed into the state over the last three or four hundred years, as individual baronial territories (and their economies) merged into nation-states. Today we are justifiably proud of having freed science, education, and cultural affairs in general from their medieval affiliation with religion. We certainly do not wish for a return to the Middle Ages. We want to move forward, not backward; but now times have changed, and it is not enough to pride ourselves on the fact that our intellectual institutions no longer serve the church. An example drawn from quite close at hand illustrates that their situation, although different today, is not necessarily more independent.

This story involves a scientist[†] whom I respect greatly; it is not intended to belittle him in any way. As the general secretary of the Prussian Academy of Science, he gave a well-received speech that described the Academy's relationship to the state, saying in effect that the members of this scholarly body deemed it their highest honor to serve as the scientific bodyguard of the House of Hohenzollern. This is only one possible example out of hundreds of thousands, and they all raise the question, what has taken the place of the church? What does public intellectual activity serve today? Until recently, the consequences of state control of education were not too bad, but they will certainly become worse if governments such as those in Eastern Europe come to power and impose their terribly regimented type of instruction, which promises to destroy all culture. If you look to the future as well as to the past, you will realize that the time has come for cultural and intellectual affairs to take their place as an independent and self-governing organ in the social organism.

Such statements encounter countless prejudices. Today, disregarding the many blessings of a government-run education system is considered a sign of insanity. These benefits will be felt, however, only when the entire education system—from kindergarten teachers to university instructors—and all related cultural affairs, become self-governing rather than being administered by the state. This is one of the major shifts we must encourage today.

The first group of people receptive to the idea of implementing social threefolding was the group that also stands behind the first truly independent comprehensive school.[†] This model school, associated with the Waldorf-Astoria factory, is based on educational theories founded on a real knowledge of the growing, developing human being. Social class and economic status make no difference in how children aged seven to fifteen should be taught, but we must be familiar with their development before we can teach them.

I became acutely aware of the extent to which we now accept state control of education as a matter of course when I had to develop the preparatory course for the faculty of the Waldorf School in Stuttgart.[†] We have no idea of all the implications of this matter-of-fact acceptance. In fact, however, state control of education has come to a head only in the last few decades. Since our actions in life must be based on experience, let me point out that I am not speaking with the flippancy of youth, but from the perspective of someone who has nearly six decades of life behind him. If you are my age, you will remember a time when the school system was still vital, the curriculum was short, and teachers had to put their own reading and experience to creative use in presenting their subject matter. Today, however, the curriculum is not short. It is a big, thick book that prescribes not only *what* to do in any given school year, but also *how* to do it. What ought to be left to teachers' initiative is increasingly being defined by law. Until we develop a clear and adequate sense of the inherently antisocial impact of state regulation of education, we will not be ready to contribute to humankind's recovery. Establishing the independence of cultural and intellectual affairs from the state is therefore the first key point in threefolding the social organism. In future, the cultural administrative organ of the social organism will preside only over active cultural workers. In a new model republic that reflects all aspects of life, instruction will bear little resemblance to that mandated by today's centralized governments. Lesson content will not be subject to regulation, but will be adapted creatively to the needs and developmental stages of the learners. We will not simply ask what young people need to learn at age thirteen or sixteen in order to become good Socialists. We will ask, what intrinsic abilities can we encourage in people of this age? What inborn forces can we help them release from the depths of their being so they will not become weak-willed, broken individuals (like so many today) but will be able to cope with their destiny and make their unique contributions to life? All this belongs to the first organ of the threefold social organism.

Of course, these ideas will initially meet with questions and objections, as I recently experienced in a city in southern Germany. During the discussion after my lecture, a university professor responded more or less as follows: "In the future, Germany will be a poor nation. You are trying to make cultural affairs independent of the state, but poor people will not be able to pay for an independent culture because they have no money. We will be forced to dip into the state's coffers after all, since taxes will have to be used to pay for the educational system. But if schools are supported by the state, how can they avoid state oversight?" I could only reply that I found it very strange that the professor believed that, in the future, tax monies would simply appear in the state's coffers without being taken from "poor people." We repeatedly encounter such careless thinking in all aspects of life. We must counteract it with a pragmatic thinking that is capable of grasping life's realities and developing practical programs that can then be implemented.

Like cultural affairs (especially the education system), the economy must also become independent. It is strange to note that two contradictory demands—namely, democracy and socialism—have recently emerged from the depths of human nature. Before the catastrophic war, these two contradictory impulses were actually welded into a single party, the Social Democrats, which is about the same as saying "wooden iron." Although socialism and democracy are incompatible, both are sincere and honest demands. Now that the catastrophic World War is over and we are faced with its aftermath, the demand for socialism has come to the fore and wants nothing to do with a democratic parliament. Socialist demands are presented with no idea of the actual realities, in the form of highly abstract slogans such as "We must seize political power" and "dictatorship of the working class." These catchwords, however, emerge from the subconscious depths of socialist sensibilities and actually prove that people are finally grasping the incompatibility of socialist and democratic sensibilities. Because the future will have to accommodate life's realities—not slogans—we will be forced to acknowledge both that socialists are right in feeling uncomfortable about democracy and that democrats are right in being horrified by the words "dictatorship of the working class."

So what are the realities of this seemingly contradictory situation? We simply need to see the state's relationship to the economy in the same way that we viewed its relationship to cultural affairs. In recent times, people in general and self-styled progressives in particular have favored increased state intervention in the economy. The postal system, communications, railroads, etc., have all come under state control and people now want to see this authority extended. Today I can devote only a few words to this very broad topic, which deserves to be presented in expert terminology and with countless examples from recent history. Due to time constraints, I run the risk of being called amateurish, which is not the case. If we take socialism seriously, however, the progressive predilection for state control will be revealed in its true colors. Even more revealing is what Friedrich Engels wrote, in one of his clearest moments, in his pamphlet *The Development of Socialism from a Utopia to a Science*.[†] He said something to the effect that if we survey recent developments in government, we will find that it has assumed control of the branches of production, of the circulation of goods, etc. While involved in this economic activity, however, the state is also involved in governing people, providing the laws that guide the economic and other actions of individuals. An economically active entity also establishes the laws governing economic behavior. In the future, this will have to change.

Engels was quite right in thinking that managing the economy would have to be separated from governing human beings, and that economic management should be responsible only for the production and circulation of goods. This view, although totally correct, is only half or perhaps a quarter of the truth, because if the state withdraws from managing the production and circulation of goods, its function of determining the terms and conditions of labor must still find a home somewhere, but this home must be found in a democratic government rather than in a centralized authoritarian state.

This means that the impulses of socialism and democracy point to two distinct remnants of the former state that must become independent organs in the social organism, along with an independent administration for cultural and intellectual affairs. One of these organs is the administrative structure of the economy; the other that of civil rights, which deals with everything individuals of voting age are free and competent to judge. Inherent in the demand for democracy is the historical fact that humankind is now maturing to the point of assuming legal responsibility (within the framework of an independent sphere of rights) for all aspects of life in which individuals are inherently equal—in other words, for everything that can be decided collectively by all individuals of legal age, either through a direct vote or through their elected representatives.

In the future, therefore, civil rights will need to be established on an independent basis. This remnant of the former authoritarian state will be the first true constitutional state under the rule of law. Its laws will apply only to those aspects of life that are legitimately subject to the collective judgment of all individuals of legal age. These aspects include a common subject of discussion among workers, but once again their words must be taken only as a social thermometer of sorts. In another statement that has made a deep impression on the hearts and minds of the working class, Karl Marx said that a humanly unworthy existence results when workers are forced to sell their labor like a commodity in the employment market.† Like any manufactured item sold for a specific price, labor is also bought and sold for a "price," i.e., a wage. In recent human affairs, this statement is less significant for its content than for its lightning-like impact on the working class, which is almost inconceivable to the leading classes.

The origin of this impact lies in the chaotic, inorganic way in which the regulation of labor has been subsumed into the business cycle and integrated into the management of legitimate economic factors, which are limited to the production, circulation, and consumption of goods. The damage will be undone only by eliminating the ability to regulate the type, scope, and duration of labor—whether intellectual or manual—from the economic cycle. Regulating labor does not belong in the economy, where wealthier individuals and groups have the power to impose terms of work on the economically disadvantaged. Regulating what one person does for another belongs in the sphere of rights, where all individuals of legal age meet as equals. Economic requirements and assumptions cannot be allowed to dictate how much work I must do for someone else. In the future, such issues will be the jurisdiction of a democratic government limited to the sphere of rights, in contrast to today's authoritarian state.

Here, too, attempts to explain this issue encounter any number of preconceived biases. It is all too easy for people to say that as long as the economy continues to be driven by free market conditions, it goes without saying that recompense for labor depends on production and on the price of goods. In the future, however, we will recognize labor (which will be subject to state regulation as a rights issue) as an inherent constraint on the economy, just like the constraints imposed by an industry's base in natural resources. We will then see the fallacy in managers' attempts to align the costs of production (which include labor) with their income projections. That would be as ridiculous as landowners getting together and looking at their account books for the year 1918 and saying, we need to produce as much this year as last year, and since it's already September, that means we will have to have so and so many days of rain and so and so many of sunshine before the end of the year. Just as agricultural prices are now determined on the basis of natural constraints, the number of hours individuals must work to support themselves will be determined on a purely democratic basis, and prices will have to be adjusted accordingly.

We must learn completely new ways of thinking instead of talking about small, incremental improvements. Economic unrest will fade away only when labor is seen as the legitimate purview of an independent, democratic common ground where all individuals of legal age meet as equals; when free individuals contribute their legally protected work to an independent economy; and when production, not labor, is governed by contractual agreements in the economic realm. This is what we need to understand.

I can only touch on this subject in the short time available today. I would like to give an entire series of lectures about it, but unfortunately that will not be possible during this visit to Berlin. Before we close, however, I must still indicate how the economy, the third organ, will take shape in the threefold social organism.

The management of capital, land, the means of production (which are also capital, by the way), and labor cannot remain part of the economy. The economy can be responsible only for managing the production, circulation, and consumption of goods. How prices are set is the germinal cell of the economy, so to speak. In a more circumscribed economy, which should be based entirely on expert knowledge and competence, how will price-setting be accomplished? It will certainly not be left to chance in the free market, as it has been so far in the national and international economies. In the context of associations between individual branches of industry and consumer cooperatives, individuals with the necessary expertise will set prices in a holistic and rational manner, avoiding the crises provoked by the haphazard effects of supply and demand. In the new economy, where determining the type and character of labor falls to the sphere of rights, what workers receive in exchange for producing goods will allow them to meet all their needs until the next production cycle is complete. The following example is rough, amateurish, and superficial, but it will have to do for today: If I make a pair of boots, the mutually agreed-upon sale price must allow me to purchase everything I need to meet my needs until I have made another pair. Of course society will have to establish organizations to ensure that the needs of widows, orphans, and the sick and disabled are met, and to provide for education and the like. The setting of equitable and realistic prices, however, which is exclusively the jurisdiction of the socially responsible economy, will depend on the formation of corporate bodies for that purpose, whether elected or appointed by joint producer-consumer associations.

Equitable price-setting must be supported by the living structure of the economy as a whole. I am not referring to the type of planned economy proposed by Moellendorff.† As an example of what I mean, let's suppose that certain manufactured items tend to become too expensive which means that too few of them are being produced. When this happens, contractual agreements must direct workers to the branches of industry that can produce these articles. Conversely, if an item becomes too inexpensive, some of the factories producing it must be idled, and their workers redirected into other branches of production. Those who reject this process as too difficult, preferring to stick with small improvements in social conditions, cannot expect real change.

Although the state has taken the economy under its wing, I have shown you how associations shaped entirely by economic forces can and must make the economy self-managing in a way that preserves individual initiative to the greatest possible extent. This cannot happen in a planned economy or through collectivization of the means of production. It can happen only through associations that develop within independent branches of industry and through their agreements with consumer cooperatives.

Until now, the leading classes have initiated the nationalization of industry. It would be a terrible mistake to take this process to the extreme. Radical collectivization would totally undermine the connection of the resulting planned economy to external economic forces. By contrast, the associations proposed by the threefolding movement are intended to preserve both the full, independent initiative of entrepreneurs and the possibility of connections between self-contained economic entities.

An independent economy will also involve changes in private property laws. Socialist theory demands the abolition of private property and its conversion to public ownership, but to informed individuals, these slogans are just meaningless words. Let me illustrate what they could mean. As you know, we are very proud of our philosophers, but our pride does not prevent sound thinking about intellectual property. We realize that intellectual property is not produced by a socialized economy or a collective, but by creative, actively involved individuals. It simply does not work to separate individuals with their abilities and talents from the process of intellectual production. Nonetheless, our thinking on this subject is socially responsible: at the end of a legally prescribed time-period after the death of the inventor or author, intellectual property no longer belongs to the heirs but enters the public domain, where it "belongs" to those who can best make it accessible to the general public. Perhaps because we place no special value on spiritual or intellectual activity, we accept time-limits on copyrights as a matter of course; but we make no attempt to deal with physical private property in the same way. Private property should also remain in the hands of its originator only as long as that person is present and applying his or her individual abilities to its management. When the original owner is no longer present, physical personal property should pass into the public domain: that is, to those with the most ability to administer it for the good of all.

This conclusion is readily evident to unbiased thinking. Take, for example, the building of our college of spiritual science, called the Goetheanum, in Dornach, near Basel, Switzerland. (We have been calling it the Goetheanum ever since the world became "Woodrow Wilsonized" and we German-speaking people needed to present our intellectual heritage boldly to the entire world. Imagine the Goetheanum as the foreign representative of Germanic culture—

that's something completely different than chauvinism!) But the point I want to emphasize is something else: The college of spiritual science that is now under construction is being managed by people with the ability to bring such a venture to life. But who will own it when these individuals are no longer among the living? It will not be bequeathed to anyone but will pass into the hands of those best able to administer it in the service of humanity. It actually "belongs" to no one.

Socially responsible economic thinking will result in future recovery. In my book *Social Renewal,* I presented further details about the transfer and circulation of private property, and demonstrated that the social organism needs to be organically subdivided into three independent but interacting organs: a self-administering cultural organ based on freedom in cultural and intellectual affairs; a democratic government that is responsible for civil rights and based on the judgment of all individuals of legal age; and an independent economy that rests on the competence and expertise of individuals and corporate entities and the mutual associations they form.

Ever since I began presenting these seemingly new and unfamiliar ideas in Germany, people have been saying that my intention was to cut the state, which needs to be a unity, into three pieces. My response was, if I say a horse has to stand on four legs, am I cutting it into four pieces? Is it a unity only if it is able to stand on one leg? It is equally silly to claim that because a human community must be a unity, all of its different aspects must merge into a single amorphous whole. In the future, we will no longer allow ourselves to be hypnotized by the abstract concept of the centralized state. We will realize that it has to stand on three legs: a self-administering cultural and intellectual system, a political structure based on democratic legislation, and an economy with its own expert administration.

More than a century ago, a half-truth was proclaimed in Western Europe and became deeply inscribed in human hearts and minds in the form of the ideals of liberty, equality, and fraternity. The people of the nineteenth century who then pointed out the basic incompatibility of these ideals were certainly not fools. They said that neither liberty nor fraternity can exist where absolute equality prevails. These objections were absolutely correct, but only because they emerged at a time when we were hypnotized by the idea of the so-called centralized state. They will no longer apply when we shake off this hypnotic trance and understand the need for a threefold subdivision of the social organism.

In conclusion, please allow me to present a comparison that illustrates issues I would have liked to discuss at greater length than was possible today. I realize that a less sketchy presentation would have been needed for you to truly understand these issues. In conclusion, however, let me mention how the centralized state "hypnotized" people who wanted it to be governed by the three great ideals of liberty, equality, and fraternity. We will have to learn to look at the state differently. At present we are accustomed to seeing the centralized state as a divinity. We are like Faust saying to sixteen-year-old Gretchen, "He who embraces and sustains all, does he not also embrace and sustain you, me, and himself?"† We relate similarly to the hypnotic idol of the centralized state. We fail to realize that it must be subdivided into three for the sake of humankind's future salvation. It is easy to imagine factory owners speaking to their employees in a semblance of Faust's words, "The state, which embraces and sustains all. Does it not also embrace and sustain itself, you, and me"—but they would have to clasp their hands over their mouths so as not to say "me" too loudly!

The necessity of threefolding the social organism must be acknowledged, especially in proletarian circles. Recognizing its necessity is crucial to understanding it. In the future, the call for "liberty, equality, and fraternity" must not ignore the inherent incompatibility of these ideals. Instead, we must recognize that *liberty* applies to the cultural and intellectual system, *equality* to all individuals of legal age in a democratic political system, and *fraternity* to a self-administering economy that nourishes and sustains individuals. As soon as we apply these three ideals to the threefold social organism in this way, they will no longer be contradictory.

May a time come when we look back on all the pain and suffering that followed Versailles and see it simply as a starting-point. May we realize that, although our outer possessions can be taken from us, we can still think back on the turn of the eighteenth to the nineteenth century and reclaim for ourselves the great intellectual property of Central Europe— the work of Lessing, Herder, Schiller, Goethe, and so on. If we do so, the hardships of our times will resound with the second half of the hundred-year-old truth of "liberty, equality, and fraternity." Although Central Europe may have lost its outer independence, these words will resound in inner freedom and independence for all the world to hear:

> Liberty in cultural affairs;
> Equality for democratically governed individuals;
> Fraternity in the economy!

These token words sum up what we must say and how we must think and feel in order to achieve a comprehensive and holistic grasp of the social issues of our time. When many people achieve this understanding, today's questions and issues will become tomorrow's practical solutions.

# 4

## SPIRITUAL SCIENCE, FREEDOM OF THOUGHT, AND SOCIETAL FORCES

### STUTTGART, DECEMBER 19, 1919

For observers of contemporary culture, it feels somewhat like an oppressive nightmare to realize how few people understand that we are on a slippery slope with regard to the most important aspects of our culture. Surely the events of recent years, which broke over us like a tidal wave, have made this fact obvious. Nonetheless, many of our contemporaries clearly believe that if we just start with our current situation, everything else will fall into place. They assume that we will be able to avoid deepening chaos without implementing comprehensive changes. Over the years, I have felt compelled to speak out against this perception, pointing repeatedly to the need to learn new ways of thinking that will motivate us to plumb the depths of our intellectual and cultural life in search of foundations for a real restructuring of public affairs. Admittedly, a small number of people are indeed aware that decisive action is needed if we are not to continue down this slippery slope. Even these few people, however, show little understanding of the reality of the situation: namely, that we must make every effort to achieve a new metamorphosis of the human spirit if we hope to heal the many pathological aspects of our declining culture.

Three phenomena shed light on the most important points for understanding our time and its needs. The first phenomenon, which I would call the principle shortcoming of our time, is inadequate insight into cultural and spiritual affairs. For decades, my lectures on spiritual science have attempted to draw attention to this shortcoming and its consequences for humanity's present and future development. The second phenomenon, which I would call the principle *demand* of our time, speaks loudly and clearly in contemporary realities. It has resounded in many hearts for over a century, ever since the words of Schiller's *Don Carlos* were first uttered: "Give me/us freedom of thought!"[†] Deeper insight into the political and cultural events of our time reveals that many social demands actually conceal a demand for the free activity of human thinking, the inmost core of our being. Many people sigh under the burden of ways of thinking derived either from outdated institutions or from recent economic circumstances. They sense that official credos or economic constraints obstruct independent thought. Their actual longing remains largely unconscious; they are aware only of a vague dissatisfaction that they cannot freely admit, namely, that they feel entitled to a more humanly worthy existence. We have implemented a great variety of social programs that are well intentioned, but are not based on insight into the human soul's most profound yearning: namely, the longing for absolute freedom of activity for the inmost core of our being—in short, freedom of thought. We sense that modern cultural, political, and economic circumstances embed us in social forces of such complexity that our intellectual understanding and our programmatic aspirations are inadequate to the task of shaping social structures such that individuals conscious of their humanity can affirm that they are leading humanly worthy lives. Mastering social forces, therefore, is the *principal need* of our time.

Because I have lectured so extensively in Stuttgart over the years, I assume that most of you are aware of the inner purpose and spirit of spiritual science, which sees itself as a cultural need of our times. I will therefore raise only a few principal points here today. By way of introduction, however, let me mention something we have already discussed here in various contexts.

Outsiders often associate spiritual science with all kinds of elusive mysticism, unsound theosophy, and the like. In spite of all our efforts to explain the true purpose of spiritual science, why is it so often interpreted as its exact opposite? The reason has to do with the fact that for three or four centuries, our lives have been increasingly shaped and dominated by a way of thinking epitomized by modern natural science. It makes no difference whether we are scientists or simple, uneducated people: whenever we seek explanations of human nature, society, or the cosmos, our thinking is modeled on natural scientific patterns of thought.

If you have often heard me lecture, you know that I do not underestimate scientific thinking. I certainly acknowledge its great triumphs, but it has achieved them—and taken hold of a large part of our life in the process—by becoming tremendously one-sided over the last three or four centuries. When we think scientifically, our knowledge is based on lifeless nature; that is, on physics and chemistry, which lead straight to technology. This same thinking underlies all of our modern institutions and even infiltrates our methods of healing and other aspects of knowledge intended to be directly helpful to human beings. But if we are unbiased in acknowledging the monumental progress of biology, physics, and chemistry, and in appreciating the scope of conscientiously applied scientific methods, we will also be fully aware of the limitations of natural scientific thinking. If we delve more deeply into what we now call "real" science, we discover that it is best at providing information about lifeless nature and the aspects of life most closely involved with lifeless matter. But when we consider the scope of natural scientific cognition, we stop short when we confront the inner nature of the human being. Without succumbing to self-deception, it is impossible to believe that the scientific views that lead so deeply into lifeless nature and produce such "great technical accomplishments" can tell us anything about human nature.

Those who do not put their faith in the *fable convenue* of outer, so-called history know that until three or four centuries ago, the inner nature of the human being was accessible to primal, instinctive knowledge. Humankind as a whole, however, develops and changes over time just as each individual does, and at the current stage of our collective evolution, this instinctive knowledge is no longer possible. Since the days of Copernicus and Galileo, we have had to investigate outer phenomena consciously. Now we must also investigate human nature consciously. At the decisive point where natural science proves incapable of insight into the essential nature of the human being, we must fall back on the intellectual modesty (as I have often called it) that is the starting point of truly human development.

Unless a genuine feeling for knowledge leads us to intellectual modesty, we will not achieve real insight into the nature of the human being. Imagine how five-year-olds relate to the contents of a book of Goethe's lyric poetry—they can do more than look at the book, or perhaps damage it. We realize that they have yet to undergo the development that allows the contents to speak to adults. Similarly, we must realize that our natural development equips us for life as little as it equips a five-year-old to deal with a volume of verse. We can, however, further our development deliberately, by applying methods that transcend those which are normally believed to be the only means possible. If we take our development into our own hands, we discover unknown forces lying hidden within us. When these forces are awakened, they can lead to a type of knowledge as rigorously scientific as any discoveries of the natural sciences. This new knowledge transcends knowledge of the outer, sense-perceptible world and leads us into the supersensible world, where we can begin to penetrate the inner nature of the human being. The first step, however, is to admit that the forces, which enable us to perceive the natural world, are inadequate for perceiving inner human nature. This higher perception requires forces that lie waiting to be brought up from the depths of the human soul. Until we make the effort, however, they are as dormant as the intellect of a five-year-old child.

Spiritual science as you know recognizes the possibility of moving from a perspective adequate for perceiving and understanding the lifeless outer world to cognitive perspectives that allow us to penetrate into the essence of being human. This science of the spirit is not the same as the idle ruminations of self-absorbed mysticism or any outer practices intended to lead to spirit. It is based entirely on real human developmental potentials similar to the inner faculties mathematicians develop. The science of spirit aims to be as strictly logical as any other branch of science, but it applies its logic only to the spiritual perception that results when dormant faculties are awakened in the human soul. My book *How to Know Higher Worlds* describes soul-spiritual practices that cultivate inner forces and open our spirit eyes and ears (to use Goethe's words)† so that we actually perceive spirit and soul, which are otherwise mere words to us. In this book, I point out the importance of cultivating and strengthening our thinking and the need for self-discipline—that is, for deliberately taking our development in hand rather than simply leaving it up to life—if we are to open our spiritual eyes and ears.

Most of our contemporaries still actively reject such ideas. We need only point out, however, that in our time social demands are emerging everywhere. At the same time, antisocial drives prevail. These antisocial drives stem from the fact that human beings pass each other by without understanding one another. And why don't we understand each other? Because what we call knowledge is all in our heads. It is limited to the intellect and does not pervade the whole person. The unique aspect of our spiritual science is that the insights provided by the forces it cultivates do pervade the whole person. They not only speak to our intellect or our heads but also pour into our feelings and our will. They imbue our feelings with understanding for the other human beings around us, and imbue our will with ethical impulses and a sense of social responsibility that also has immediate practical impacts.

An unfortunate distinction between intellectual and manual work is currently being proclaimed on every street corner. What is manual work? Nothing more or less than applying our bodily instruments in the service of our will. We will understand the inmost impulses of spiritual science, however, only when we keep the whole person in mind and realize—as I have so often said—that our will is a spiritual element that pulses in everything we do as whole human beings and reflects back into our reason or our heads.

I hope you will forgive me for mentioning several personal examples at this point. I do so only because they will help clarify the objective state of affairs. As you know, the Goetheanum that is under construction on a hill in Dornach, Switzerland, in the Jura Mountains, is intended to become a college of spiritual science. When we started planning the college and its building, it was out of the question to consult any architect who worked from an outdated architectural or artistic perspective. This building, dedicated to the pursuit of spiritual science, required a different approach. From the very beginning, our spiritual science has proven capable of involvement in all the outer manifestations of culture. It is truly able to revive and fructify our dated art and architecture, as well as our working life and practical affairs. Clearly, we could not simply hire someone to construct a building in the Greek, Romanesque, Gothic, or any other style. Spiritual science itself gave rise to the architectural ideas of what the building would have to look like in every line and form.[†] Even in its smallest details, it is a visible crystallization of the ethos of spiritual science.

But to return to the personal examples: in the fall and winter of 1913-1914, I built a detailed model of the entire building. Even the architectural drawings were based on it. So was that manual labor or intellectual labor? In this case, the two coalesced and functioned as a unity. I know this because I did it. Then, again, there is also almost nothing in the building that I have not had a hand in, like any other worker. And you might also be interested to know that we are working on a nine-and-a-half meter high wooden statue—an artistic representation of the human riddle of our time—to serve as the focal point of the interior. The work is artistic, but it resembles nothing as much as chopping wood, if I may say so myself, and I have calluses on my fingers to show that the creative intellectual work that takes place there from morning to night involves real hands-on activity. And the final example: a short time ago we had to come to a financial decision about whether to make or purchase chairs. The bid we received was outrageously high, so, together with one of our exceptionally skillful workers, we made a sample chair in our art studio. When it was done, there was no way of telling where the intellectual work left off and the manual work began. (By the way, those chairs will cost only forty percent of what we would have had to pay the bidder.)

Our group of coworkers consists partly of employees and partly of friends of our movement. For example, there is one woman, a certified medical assistant, who sharpens chisels for our sculpture work from morning till night. In the working relationships in this group, there is actually only one obstacle that prevents intellectual work from merging seamlessly with manual work to the complete satisfaction of workers of both types. That obstacle is the organization that exists among the employees, who view everything the intellectual workers do with mistrust even though both groups are actually doing the same work.

What caused this deep abyss that separates the inner work of art, science, and political intellectual leadership from the outer work performed primarily by the working class? The reason is that everything relating to the human being as a whole has been eliminated from our thinking. Healing this abyss is possible only through spiritual science, not through any unsound, one-sided mysticism or theosophy that people of leisure cultivate without developing any practical impetus. Spiritual science fosters healing by involving the whole person. Having said this, let me add that I am certain that the knowledge I now represent before the world in full responsibility would never have come to me if I had not had to spend my entire life doing things that would ordinarily be considered manual work—because that kind of work also has specific effects on a person. So-called mental work that engages only the intellect does not reach the spirit. Today we think of manual labor or practical work as "out there" and mental, intellectual work as "in here." Nothing could be farther from the truth. As paradoxical as it may sound to many people today, the separation between practical work and so-called intellectual work developed because both are devoid of spirit. Either we are stuck on the mechanistic treadmill of technology, as workers standing in front of machines and applying our intellect exclusively to the performance of mechanical tasks; or we are educated for intellectual activity and are insufficiently involved in real, practical work. Our intellectual activity is as devoid of spirit as our practical activity. Spirit will be present in our thoughts only when they are fully saturated with reality, when we are harmoniously involved in the world as whole individuals, and when we think not merely with our heads but as people who touch and shape things with their hands and notice how practical activity reflects back into the head. The products of disconnected thinking are as devoid of spirit as any products of machines.

Spiritual science as we know it must not engage in a form of mysticism that is remote from everyday life, but must grow out of full involvement in life. In comparison to the usual intellectual and cultural activity of today, spiritual science must be much more completely saturated with reality. But can we actually call our contemporary intellectual culture "saturated with reality"? Don't we see that our science is powerless to grasp the spirit? In our culture, we usually think we are involved in unbiased scientific activity. This "unbiased" science, however, came about over the course of several centuries when social conditions allowed the religious denominations to monopolize everything that people wanted to know about soul and spirit, about the life that transcends birth and death. We were allowed to think independently about the outer, sense-perceptible world, but not about soul and spirit. As we adapted to this centuries-long ban on soul and spirit research, our scientists became accustomed to limiting their thinking and investigation to the sense-perceptible world. Ultimately, through an elaborate process of self-deception, they arrived at the conviction that exact science was inherently limited to studying the outer, sense-perceptible world and that soul and spirit research went beyond the limits of human cognition. This idea took root in modern sensibilities until it pervaded all aspects of our life. Such a limited approach allows fruitful thinking about the natural world, but proves inadequate as soon as it is applied to human society. To establish genuine social sciences with a real impact on life would require imbuing ourselves with a holistic view of the human being. The influences I have just described have prevented us from developing such a view.

That is how we came to accept spirit and soul as merely the fixed outcomes of centuries of dogma rather than as legitimate subjects for research. Spirit and soul hover over "real life" like so much smoke and fog, and we have come to view reality as if shaped exclusively by economic forces. We have ceased to believe that spirit works in economic forces, and this disbelief has led to the disastrous conviction that spiritual, cultural, and intellectual life will develop on their own, out of purely economic forces, if those forces are simply organized appropriately. We lack any insight that economic phenomena were originally manifestations of spiritual activity. We also fail to realize that our culture has become estranged from the real world. Its recovery will require a real science of spirit capable of understanding human beings as fully and completely as the natural sciences understand machines. This science of spirit, however, must be based on the cultivation of forces in human nature. To put it briefly, it has become extremely difficult to recognize that spiritual science must become the foundation for understanding and mastering societal issues. The human intellect seems to lack the impetus to delve into real life, and as a consequence our lives will become increasingly chaotic unless our feelings and will are stimulated by other impulses that allow individuals to relate to each other on a one-to-one basis and to shape and direct social forces. No matter what methods you adopt from our exact and exemplary natural sciences, you will not be able to develop social sciences on the same basis. Trying to apply to the social sciences perceptions and ideas acquired without benefit of the insights of spiritual science is like trying to apply paint to a greased surface. Paint will not adhere to a greasy surface, and neither will merely intellectual science adhere to real life.

Our public life is crying out for a deepening that spiritual science can provide. Spiritual science will have to provide the foundation for resolving the unconscious contents of modern social demands. The actual demands cannot be formulated because the requisite power of thinking is not available to people. That is why we must not see spiritual science as something to which we devote a few passing thoughts. In fact, it is one of the most necessary prerequisites for the recovery of our public life. As a pragmatist, I know what people will say—that they have jobs; they have to work; and they don't have enough time to devote to something as complex as spiritual science. On the other hand, no matter how busy we are today, we cannot avoid noticing that we are treading on a slippery slope. Does what we are busy doing simply help lead the way into chaos? Don't we really need to devote every hour we can spare to radical prospects for recovery?

Spiritual science, as we know and practice it, is intimately related to the century-old cry for freedom of thought, which is actually a cry for social freedom. Strangely enough, when we now attempt to examine what the stormy surges of so-called social demands bring to the surface, we repeatedly collide with the need to truly understand the impulse of human freedom, which manifests in different ways. We touch on an important point here—a point acknowledged even by Woodrow Wilson, whom I consider the most hapless of all the influential and so-called outstanding individuals of our times.† Since I never spoke differently about Woodrow Wilson even during the war (on neutral ground), when he was being worshipped everywhere, I suppose I can continue in a similarly uncomplimentary vein. Many passages in Wilson's book *The New Freedom†* suggest that social conditions can be improved only by taking people's quest for freedom seriously. (Obviously, he is primarily aware of conditions in America.) But what does human freedom mean to him?

Here we come upon a very interesting chapter in modern thinking. (Wilson is, after all, a representative thinker of sorts.) Writing on freedom, he expresses the following view: We can get an idea of freedom by looking at how a gear functions in a machine. If the mechanical device operates freely and without hindrance, we say that the gear moves freely. Similarly, a ship's machinery must be adapted to the motion of the waves so the waves help propel the boat forward freely rather than obstructing its progress. Wilson then compares what the impulse of human freedom ought to be to a gear in a machine or a ship in the ocean waves, claiming that human beings are free when they move forward freely in the context of outer circumstances, when their forces are integrated into outer forces and are not obstructed.

I find it very interesting that this strange view of human freedom should emerge from our modern scientific way of thinking. Isn't it the opposite of freedom when you are so completely adapted to outer circumstances that you can only move with them, not against them? Doesn't freedom demand the ability to resist outer circumstances when necessary? Wouldn't we have to compare freedom to something that allows the ship to turn against the waves and stop, if necessary?

This strange view will never lead to sound diplomatic insight. At best, it can lead only to Wilson's abstract Fourteen Points, at least some of which have been favorably received even in this country. But where does this view come from? It comes from our failure to realize that, to truly speak of freedom, we must return to human thought as such, which is the only thing that can possibly provide a real impulse for freedom in our life. This is the idea I attempted to present thirty years ago in *The Philosophy of Freedom*, which has recently appeared in a new and updated edition. In that book, I attempted to formulate the human impulse for freedom in a way that is different from the prevailing modern conception. I attempted to show that we are asking the wrong questions about human freedom. We ask: Are human beings free or not free? Are we beings who can freely make decisions and take responsibility for them, or are we creatures of nature, tied to natural or spiritual inevitabilities? People have asked these questions for millennia and are still asking them today, but these are the wrong questions.

Our questions about freedom are actually questions about human development, the development we undergo in adolescence (or even later in life) in order to acquire inner forces not provided by nature. We cannot ask: are human beings free? In terms of what nature gives us, we are not free, but we can become increasingly free by awakening forces that lie dormant within us, forces that nature does not awaken for us. The appropriate question is not whether human beings are free, but simply, is there a way for human beings to acquire freedom? And yes, there is a way.

Thirty years ago, I attempted to show that when we progress to the point of developing an inner life in which we grasp the ethical motivation for our actions in pure thoughts, we can then attribute our actions to real thought-impulses, not simply to instinctive emotions. Such thoughts merge with outer reality as lover and beloved become one. When this happens, we approach freedom. Freedom, therefore, is as much the child of thought (conceived in spiritual clairvoyance rather than under outer duress) as the child of true, devoted love for the object of one's actions. This is what German culture was striving for through Schiller when he opposed Kant and sensed something of this freedom. We would do well to continue to cultivate it today. It became apparent to me, however, that we can speak only about what underlies moral actions—a foundation that does exist, although people remain unconscious of it—and that we must call it "intuition." This is the "moral intuition" of *The Philosophy of Freedom*.

This was the starting point for everything I later attempted to accomplish in the field of spiritual science. Please don't think that I am being immodest. I am well aware that this book, which I wrote thirty years ago as a young man, suffered from all the childhood diseases of nineteenth-century thinking, so to speak. But I also know that the intellectual life of the nineteenth century also planted the seeds of a type of thinking that leads to the spirit. I realized that when human beings rise to ethical impulses in moral intuition as truly free beings, they are already "clairvoyant"—to use a much-maligned word—with regard to their ethical intuitions. The impulses for all ethical activity transcend sense-perceptible reality. Fundamentally, truly ethical imperatives are products of human clairvoyance. In this sense, there is a straight line from *The Philosophy of Freedom* to today's spiritual science. Freedom emerges only in human beings who cultivate their own development. As this development continues and we extend the foundations of freedom, however, we can become independent of any ethical system and rise freely into domains of spirit.

Freedom, therefore, is associated with the development of human thinking. Essentially, freedom is always freedom of thought, and when we look at representative individuals such as Woodrow Wilson, we realize that they come up with paradoxical definitions (like Wilson's definition of freedom, for example) because they have never grasped that thinking must be rooted in real spirit if it is not to become abstract. Examples such as this reveal the *principle shortcoming* of our modern intellectual culture, which consists in not discerning the spiritual nature of the human being. We then also recognize freedom of thought as the *principle demand* of our time and mastering social forces as its *principle need*. Now, and in the near future, our life must move toward providing a foundation for these three principle phenomena. The primal human impulse of freedom cannot be found in any aspect of human nature that is accessible to natural scientific thinking, but only in the aspect accessible to spirit perception.

Freedom has been the subject of much contention because people want to make decisions about it without so much as setting foot on the ground that supports insight into the immortal nature of the human soul. But without an unbiased approach to thinking about human immortality, we are in no position to consider the essence of human freedom. We will not discover the essential character of this freedom if we seek it anywhere else than in a type of thinking that is not "natural." Once found, however, it fills individuals with the impulse to become truly socially responsible beings, inserting us into the social order in a way that releases social forces from within, which is exactly what we need.

I mentioned earlier that, during the construction of our building in Dornach, people who have actually achieved certain heights of spiritual training volunteered for very ordinary, dirty work and proved no less competent in that regard than people we normally call manual laborers. Admittedly, the Goetheanum is a symbol or representation of our spiritual-scientific movement, and the social basis of its construction is not exactly that of a for-profit venture. *Social Renewal* and my lectures on the threefold social organism present the possibility of creating similar foundations for all of our public life. It is simply a shame, however, that many people in other countries cannot visit the building because crossing national borders is impossible at the moment.

Why has an anthroposophical group managed to free up social forces that allow the proletarian ideal to be realized, although not in the way it is usually conceived? Because everything we are doing in Dornach, down to the last detail, rests on a holistic approach to life derived from spiritual-scientific impulses. The basis of what we are doing there on a small scale could also be applied to all public life. Every factory, every bank, every entrepreneurial venture, all aspects of practical life could be reorganized on the basis of a science that uses the methods I have described to penetrate deeply enough into the essence of human nature to grasp living realities, instead of abstract thoughts and abstract natural laws. We are not looking for abstract mysticism but for facts that ground us in life's realities. By recognizing the essential nature of the human being, spiritual science also discovers social forces that enable us to organize life in ways that would allow everyone to lead a humanly worthy existence.

Therefore, social forces, freedom of thought, and spiritual science are all related. Spiritual science is the exact opposite of what it is often believed to be. It is not something dreamed up by idle bystanders or people of leisure. It aims to be the truly practical approach to life that is so sadly lacking in our time. It aims to immerse itself in life, mastering it through science and practical activity. It deals with human realities, not simply life as we imagine it to be.

Today there are perfectly well-meaning people who realize that the intellect and reason we have cultivated for the last few centuries are inadequate to restore health to our public life. If you ask these people what *would* be adequate, they give abstract answers about re-enlivening "soul" with "spirit," but they come up with the strangest excuses for rejecting real spiritual science. Essentially, they are afraid of it. We repeatedly hear statements like "Not everyone can become a spiritual researcher." That is indeed true, as I have repeatedly emphasized here, but it is quite possible for everyone to take the first steps into the spiritual worlds of supersensible existence, as described in *How to Know Higher Worlds* and in the second part of *Esoteric Science*. Anyone can take these preliminary steps at any time, but progressing to a deeper understanding of the beings of the supersensible worlds depends on various experiences for which some people today are not yet ready. Becoming a spiritual researcher in the truest sense of the word involves overcoming many obstacles. For example, when body-free cognition sets in, we enter a world that is totally unfamiliar. All of our ordinary supports—the security of experiencing the sense-perceptible world, our ordinary intellect, and so on—all disappear, and we must be guided by different, inner forces. It is like hanging over the edge of a cliff and having to rely entirely on your own inner being's center of gravity. Many people are afraid of this situation, either consciously or unconsciously, and they disguise their fear in logical objections to spiritual science. They give you all kinds of nice reasons, but the truth is that they are simply afraid of the unknown.

We must also consider, however, that we are naturally adapted only to life in the outer, sense-perceptible world. The habits we acquire there do not equip us to face the spiritual world, which is completely different. Consequently, when we attempt to delve deeper into that world, we undergo terribly painful experiences. Once we overcome such obstacles, insights emerge from the depths of our being, and we learn about the eternal aspect of human nature and the spirit that underlies the entire world. Not everyone can come this far on the path to spiritual knowledge. But as I have emphasized repeatedly, it is not necessary to be a spiritual researcher oneself in order to assess the legitimacy of statements about worlds we still do not know. Healthy commonsense, unbiased by outer perception, is sufficient for distinguishing whether someone is speaking logically or as a spiritist of some sort. Logic is available to all of us, and it is all we need to tell whether someone is describing spiritually healthy experiences.

People repeatedly point out that anyone can become convinced of the accuracy of natural scientific claims simply by paying attention to the scientists' laboratory methods. It is equally correct to say that anyone can be convinced of the truth of the contents of *How to Know Higher Worlds* or *Theosophy*, because the character and qualities of spiritual researchers allow us to draw conclusions about the inherent merit of their insights. If we can acknowledge their value, these insights and their applications to life are worth as much to us as they are to those who have achieved them personally. We use outer facts to confirm the findings of natural science. Similarly, healthy commonsense can assess the manner in which insights are presented, and in this way we can use it to confirm the statements of spiritual researchers.

Just imagine the social forces that will be released as more and more people bear witness to spiritual forces, which are discovered only by spiritual researchers in supersensible worlds but can be accepted by other people who simply rely on their own healthy common sense. (After all, not everyone can become a chemist or a physicist, either.) The public social interactions that arise out of a spiritual-scientific view of the human being speak for themselves and awaken forces of trust in our public life. At present, such trust is still undermined by the fact that individuals, who have not taken their own development in hand and can barely be considered adults, feel entitled to pass judgment on anything and everything. We founded the Waldorf School, which was made possible by our dear friend Mr. Emil Molt, as an example of a school system based on true insight and as a demonstration of how spiritual science truly can supply practical impulses for public life. We are attempting to solve a social problem in the right way. Our goal is for every child to grow up to be an adult who can receive the guiding forces needed for fruitful participation in public life. These forces will not come from the boring, inaccessible knowledge often propounded by the social thinkers of our time. In its place, we are attempting to foster real, socially-responsible thinking based on human trust and the secure foundations of the human soul. We see each child in this school as a human being in progress whose development can be helped along by insights that fundamentally enliven our methods of instruction. Here, as in all of its experimental practical applications, spiritual science shows us what is needed.

In one lecture, of course, I am limited to only a couple of the possible perspectives on spiritual science as a necessary challenge to contemporary and future developments. These inherently one-sided indications are easy to oppose because they cannot show the whole picture. Before we close, however, I would like to go back to the beginning and reiterate how few people recognize that our culture is on a slippery slope. The general failure to seek a basis for rebuilding our intellectual, ethical, and general cultural life weighs heavily on my heart.

Many examples exist, and I will mention a few before concluding. What conclusions do people active in public affairs draw from the realities of our present situation? There is one passage in the most recent book by the Austrian statesman Czernin† that deserves to be taken to heart (although, as for the rest of the book, you can take it or leave it):

> The great drama that has dominated the world for the last five years continues, although in a different form. I believe future generations will refer to it as the World Revolution, not the World War, recognizing that the war was only the beginning of the revolution. The treaties of Versailles and Saint-Germain will have no lasting effect. This peace harbors the destructive seed of death. The struggles that convulse Europe are not abating. Subterranean rumbling continues, as if in a massive earthquake, and from time to time the earth will break open and spew fire into the sky. Outbreaks of elemental violence will repeatedly

devastate the nations of Europe until all reminders of the insanity
of this war have been swept away. Slowly and under unspeakable
sacrifices, a new world will be born. Future generations will look
back on our century as a protracted bad dream. Even the darkest
night, however, is followed by a new day. Generations have gone
to the grave through murder, starvation, or illness. Millions of
people with hatred and murder in their hearts have died in efforts
to annihilate and destroy, but new generations are arising, and
a new spirit rises with them. Every winter is followed by spring.
Resurrection follows death: that is an eternal law in the cycle of
life. Blessed are those called to service in building up the new
world.

So Czernin also speaks of a new spirit, but I know he would reject
our new spirit as a phantasmagoria. People talk about "new spirit" in
abstract terms, but they take to their heels at the concrete prospect
of spirit. Nevertheless, tracing the path of this new, concrete spirit
is a serious matter. Today many people attack spiritual science from
the perspective of their idea of Christianity, refusing to acknowledge
that spiritual science also offers a vital foundation for re-enlivening
Christianity. In the Christianity of the future, we will rediscover the
living Christ, as well as the historic reality of the events of Golgotha,
through spiritual-scientific research. By now, a majority of theologians turn the Christ into the "simple man from Nazareth" and no
longer teach that he is the actual central meaning of earthly existence.
Spiritual science will provide a new basis for Christian spirituality. To
Christians who fear the impact of spiritual science, we should say that
the foundation of Christianity is so solid that it has nothing to fear
from spiritual science. Just as it had no reason to fear the invention
of the air pump or similar devices, it has no reason to fear spiritual-
scientific teachings on destiny or repeated earthly lives. Christianity is
strong enough to absorb anything that comes from spiritual science.
(Whether modern supporters of the Christian denominations are
equally strong is a different question, albeit a serious one.)

The so-called World War drummed into us the need for an international perspective. In thinking about Europe and our European

culture, many people echo the thoughts of a Japanese diplomat,[†] an educated man, who said:

> For a number of years, we in Japan believed in the existence of justice in the Western, Christian world. Recent years have taught us that it does not exist. The high-sounding teachings and explanations of Christian nations are nothing more than an insolent mask that conceals their injustice and greed. We now know that there is no such thing as international justice, and we also know that only superior might can contain the capitalist power of the West. Japan has learned this, and the rest of Asia is in the process of learning it. Our China policy is explained by the fact that we know we cannot count on justice or honorable dealings on the part of the Western powers. They will divide and destroy China and then reduce Japan to vassalage. They will do so without conscience, consideration, or hesitation, if we in Japan do not maintain our dominance and support and develop China ourselves. Ultimately, Western exploitation would be the ruin of China, and our policy its deliverance. In China and our Pacific territories, we must be fully equipped to defend ourselves adequately. For us to trust an Anglo-Saxon federation or to believe in any latent (let alone prevailing) justice in Christian civilization would be proof that we are idiots who deserve the destiny of national ruin, which we would inevitably face at the hands of the Western powers.

Whatever we may think of these words, they reveal how the world thinks about us, and we have every reason to regard them as fact.

Especially when they come from people who actually ought to be aware of what our spiritual culture demands, repeated objections to my efforts to present a new spirituality are truly misplaced. I mean objections such as "it is impossible to confirm what spiritual researchers say." For example, a man who lives not far from here recently published a brochure entitled *Rudolf Steiner: Philosopher and Theosophist*.[†] I would like to make only one point with regard to the spirit and logic of his remarks. He says, "Under certain circumstances,

I would have to be a historian, a physicist, or a chemist in order to test their ideas for myself. I cannot confirm theosophical truths, however, if I am not clairvoyant." Of course! I also cannot confirm the results of chemists' research without becoming a chemist myself, which I could conceivably do. But people do not want to make the effort to become spiritual scientists. In effect, this man is saying something very strange: I need to be able to confirm these statements without learning to apply relevant methods of testing. For him, the question is not whether it is *possible* to determine the validity of a statement after having acquired the basis for making the determination, but whether he has or could have made that determination *himself*. "All formal, logical criticism aside, I must answer that question in the negative." I readily admit that *he* has to answer it in the negative. But just as I recognize the need to become a chemist myself in order to confirm the results of chemists' research, anyone who wants to check the validity of spiritual-scientific truths must take steps to become a spiritual researcher, which this man refuses to do. His entire booklet is full of this logic, which also underlies many misrepresentations of spiritual science. We have better things to do than to worry about objections of this sort.

It would, however, be fitting for the much-tested German people to reassess their relationship to the actual foundations of our culture. Let me quote a few sentences from an essay on Schiller and Goethe, written in 1858 by the brilliant art historian Hermann Grimm.[†] Over sixty years ago, Grimm said, "The true history of Germany is the history of national cultural movements. Great and illuminating deeds occur only when enthusiasm for great thoughts arouses the nation and sets moribund forces in motion." Shouldn't we take these words to heart today? And what about these other words that Grimm—surely no revolutionary—wrote in 1858? He said, "The milestones of the people's progress are not the names of German Kaisers and kings," but deeds in the domain of thought that approaches spirit.

At no point in time has it ever been more necessary for Germans to accept and act on Grimm's assessment than now, in this time of need and severe tribulation. We must urge our contemporaries to look back on our great forebears so we may become their worthy successors. Are we to believe that our forefathers' confessions of faith in our culture are no longer valid today? Must we not continue their efforts rather than merely quoting their words? Quoting Goethe is not the same as understanding him; we understand him only if we continue his efforts. It is nonsense to quote Johann Gottlieb Fichte today without also carrying on his cultural efforts. You have heard what the world thinks of German culture. The rest of the world must recognize that Germans again have the will to look back on the real milestones in their progress as a people. Our forebears, the great pillars of German culture, were often called dreamers. They were misjudged just as any talk of spirit is misjudged today. Nonetheless, there were people who understood the connection between spiritual striving and reality. At an important moment, Johann Gottlieb Fichte said something to this effect: "Other people say that ideals cannot intervene directly in practical matters. We idealists know that, too, perhaps better than they do, but we also know that our life must take its direction from ideals. Those who do not realize this are not included in the world's plan for humanity. We can only hope that they will also be granted sunshine and rain at the appropriate times, along with good digestion and—if possible—a few good thoughts."[†]

Much depends on the spirit in which we now look up to the activity of the great pillars of those who gave birth to German culture. Reality, not abstract judgment, will determine the outcome. If we, as descendents of these cultural forebears, learn to appreciate genuine spiritual practice, our predecessors will not have been the dreamers the world believed them to be. But they will indeed go down in history as dreamers, if we, or our descendants, choose to remain ignorant of the real German spirit and neglect to come to grips with the realities of spiritual practice. May the German people honor the spirit invoked by German culture and thus avoid condemning their cultural forebears to this ignominious fate!

That is all I wanted to say to you today.

# 5

## The Assets and Liabilities
## of World Cultures

STUTTGART, DECEMBER 27, 1919

T HESE days, individual countries and ethnic territories are largely
cut off from each other and international travel has become difficult
or even, in some cases, impossible. If we are even somewhat involved
in modern culture, we must recognize that this state of affairs is
virtually impossible to reconcile with the deepest inner longings of
individuals. To an unbiased view, each human psyche incorporates
the spiritual and cultural strivings of all civilized peoples. To use a
financial metaphor, no one on Earth today would be able to draw up
an individual cultural balance sheet without including entries from all
over the world. But what does the balance sheet of German culture
look like right now? It is time to talk seriously about our culture's
assets and liabilities.

I hope, after the events of recent years, that I will not be misunderstood when I remind you of what the brooding, deeply digging,
thinker Friedrich Nietzsche wrote in *The Birth of Tragedy* in 1871.
The young Nietzsche, reflecting on the moods passing through his
soul in the year of Germany's unification, declared the imminent
extirpation of the German spirit in favor of the German Reich.[†] For
many of the intervening years, such a declaration must have sounded
frivolous to many people. Now, however, the realities of our situation
have changed, and regardless of whether we think Nietzsche was right

or not, his opinion—expressed at the dawning of the new German Empire by someone who had truly suffered under nineteenth-century materialism—remains significant. Perhaps we may be permitted to expand upon the idea or perception that led to this opinion. Is it possible, for example, that the German people's current disastrous situation could restore the collective soul and spirit that Nietzsche feared had been extirpated?

These introductory words were simply meant to indicate the gravity of any general observations of modern soul-spiritual life and its challenges. Although Nietzsche shed only a fleeting light on the modern cultural balance sheet in 1871, many nineteenth-century German thinkers attempted to address it seriously and conscientiously. I could list a number of such individuals, but I will mention only David Friedrich Strauss, whose materialism made him unpopular with many. Those of you who have followed my lectures over the decades will have some sense of my inner aversion to Strauss' *The Old Faith and the New.*† Nonetheless, Strauss must be given credit for unrelentingly raising the major theological issues of the mid-1800s with questions such as: Do we still have religion? Are we still Christians? As in previous instances, I do not want to give yes or no answers to these questions today, nor do I want to pass judgment on Strauss. I simply want to point out that in spite of his materialism and the trivialities Nietzsche perceived in his world-view, David Friedrich Strauss was essentially honest in what he wrote.

Strauss absorbed the nineteenth century's scientific mindset and approach to life in its entirety. He drew on the most modern intellectual accomplishments, right up to Darwin and Haeckel, to shape his inner convictions and world-view. Then, with relentless honesty, he asked: If I accept a worldview in line with modern sensibilities, can I still be religious in the old sense? Can I still be a Christian? For himself, Strauss answered both of these questions with an honest "No." That is his personal bottom-line in the balance sheet of modern soul-spiritual life.

Although, as supporters of spiritual science we must speak out emphatically against David Friedrich Strauss' credo, we must nonetheless acknowledge that he and many others arrived at an honest bottom-line. Unfortunately, the same cannot be said of all similar efforts since the mid-1800s. At every turn, the representatives of various confessions seem to be attempting to obscure the issue. On the one hand, their words are full of concessions to scientific sensibilities; on the other, they continue to talk about Christianity and religion in the same old habitual terms, with none of the forthrightness of a David Friedrich Strauss. It does not occur to them to calculate a bottom line or even to include all necessary entries in the cultural and spiritual balance sheet of our time. Obfuscation is the signature of many modern cultural trends.

Attempts by small groups to arrive at an honest bottom line do not offer an effective response to this situation, but simply lead us in circles. Comfortably clinging to little thoughts is exactly what kept us from developing a viable relationship to international realities and ultimately led to the terrible catastrophe of recent years. These horrific experiences ought to teach humankind that it is truly time to wake up and discover points of view that can teach us to manage our life consciously, instead of unconsciously allowing ourselves to be led around by the nose.

Today, there is no shortage of idealistic programs and associations. They proliferate like brambles because our wide-ranging intellect always allows us to come up with something reasonable to say, which we then swear on as if it were Holy Scripture. Supporters of these various political, cultural, ethical, or social programs always think that their idea of what is right for humanity needs to be implemented immediately and universally—in America, Europe, Asia, and all over the globe. Very often they also think that whatever they have dreamed up will remain the absolute salvation of the whole world for all time to come.

This absolutist thinking is both the fate and the cardinal sin of our modern intellectualism, which prefers not to look at the concrete human condition or how it differs between the East and the West, to give an example. Today, speaking from this perspective, I will briefly address the international cultural balance sheet by drawing attention to characteristic difference between the world-views produced by human souls in the East and West. Here in Central Europe, we have been heavily influenced by the Middle East over the centuries and millennia. On the other hand, we have been equally influenced by a newer element that has been arising in the West for some time. When we consider the foundations of Central Europe's cultural development, we turn first to Christianity, the most powerful of all impulses in humankind's earthly evolution and in Western culture in particular. Although Christianity soon moved westward to Europe, it emerged first in the Middle East. Essentially, therefore, the Christ impulse constitutes an eastern influence on the European psyche. Even today, as the poignant writings of Rabindranath Tagore[†] confirm, the entire character or structure of Eastern spiritual life points back to ancient times.

In Asia, the life of soul and spirit has always been paramount and has developed in a straight line from antiquity to the present day. Inasmuch as this Eastern spiritual life has also been instilled in our culture, it behooves us to make a profound inner effort to understand Eastern aspirations and especially the ancient, mighty sources of modern spirituality in the East. This spirituality is now in a stage of decadence or decline. Today, even the products of the best Eastern minds can scarcely be compared to the profound, meaningful spiritual life that Asia once produced for all of humankind. The further back we go, the more apparent the fundamental character of Eastern culture becomes. When we thoroughly examine everything we know about this culture, we realize that it does not originate in the soul-constitution and attitudes we now consider normal in the West. The soul-forces involved in the creation of this culture are different from the ones we ourselves apply in our advanced scientific and intellectual efforts. To really sense the character and structure of Eastern culture—although, as I said, it is now in decline—we must ask a question that I have often posed and attempted to answer on the basis of spiritual science. That question is: Does a higher nature speak through human beings without making use of the instruments of the sensory-nervous system (or of the body in general), which is what we use in our Western sciences and arts?

In lectures here in Stuttgart, I have often described spiritual-scientific methods that are as rigorous as any of the methods of modern natural science. These spiritual techniques lead spirit researchers to the eternal, immortal aspect of the human being, which enters the inherited body through conception and birth and returns to the spiritual world when the individual passes through the portal of death. What speaks to us through Eastern culture, especially its older elements, is this immortal aspect—not the aspect of ourselves that makes use of the instruments of the body and speaks through our Western science, literature, and art. The spiritual life of the East reveals what we bring with us into physical existence through conception and birth. In a certain sense, we cannot apply this spiritual aspect of ourselves here on earth, but must take it back through the portal of death. To educated Asians, real spiritual culture emanates from the higher human being within (if I may use a somewhat trite expression), that is, from something that far transcends the everyday human being.

To get a more complete idea of how those in the East related to their spiritual life in its time of flourishing, we must consider the ethical impulses we apply in the activity of distinguishing the morally right from the morally wrong. These ethical impulses appear in us as intuitions when we summon up the best forces of our inner being. We must imagine the soul-forces we then experience as extending over everything they sense and feel as they conjure up their spiritual-cultural life in the physical world. There is nothing here of the sensibilities that pervade our Western sciences, philosophies, worldviews, and superficial absolutist ideas. Instead, the Eastern worldview is imbued with an awareness of receiving a transcendent, supersensible element.

For a long time now, we in the West have not known how to relate to the supersensible world (or its manifestations in the sense-perceptible world) in this way. The so-called "higher being" within the ordinary human being appears in our outward morality in abstract terms, but the mighty, immediate experience of how this higher being creates a spiritual culture that is the direct expression of supersensible worlds has been largely lost to Western culture. Today, we ought to honestly acknowledge this liability in our cultural balance sheet.

Now let's look at individual manifestations. On the one hand, we see how the Christ impulse (as I said) flowed into all of Western culture. Its impact on Western life was once tremendous; but it has lost this impetus. In early Christian times, people who were serious about deepening their Christian worldview attempted to apply supersensible knowledge to understanding the figure of the Christ. By contrast, in the nineteenth century, the most progressive theologians and faithful Christians were very proud of eliminating the supersensible aspects of Christ Jesus. There were (and still are) university professors of Christian theology who are proud of seeing Christ Jesus only as the "simple man from Nazareth," and go to great lengths to avoid reference to his supernatural character. Even with regard to Western humanity's holiest convictions and often even among our leading thinkers, any sense of the supersensible has gradually evaporated. We no longer know what to do with centuries of developments based on an infusion of spirit from the East. We have made even our religious heritage materialistic. The most significant phenomenon here is that theology has made Christianity materialistic. It is sheer materialism to eliminate the super-earthly Christ Being who united with the personality of Jesus of Nazareth, and to consider only the personal attributes of this Jesus, as we do with any other historic figure.

Other examples also reveal this strange relationship between the Western and the Eastern mind. Many people—whether consciously or unconsciously, with good intentions or bad—confuse our anthroposophically oriented spiritual science with the theosophy of Blavatsky and Besant.[†] The point I want to emphasize today, however, is not the relationship between Anthroposophy and Theosophy, but a small but nonetheless remarkable phenomenon in the culture of a Western imperialist nation—namely, the English Theosophical movement. Theosophy's purpose in this eminently Western culture was to deepen spiritual life and re-enliven the search for the sources of spiritual experience. How did it do this? In their quest for sources of spirit, the citizens of this nation of conquerors turned to the conquered people of India and appropriated their ancient Eastern wisdom. Because we in Central Europe chose not to do likewise, the Theosophical Society branded us as heretics.[†] Compared to the former living wisdom of India, the "ether body" and the "astral body," which the English theosophists borrowed from the now decadent Indian tradition, were materialistic interpretations of what the East conceives in purely spiritual terms. This example, however, is also characteristic in another way. The Western culture epitomized by England gave its members so little basis for seeking the sources of a new spiritual life that they were forced to borrow from decadent Eastern spiritual culture and bring it home to the West. This example exemplifies Western culture's inability to give birth to the higher, spiritual, eternal human being, which dwells within the mortal body and manifests in the spiritual culture of the East. Asians are eminently aware of the higher human being who inhabits not only the earthly world, but also the spiritual worlds that transcend the earthly plane, if I may attempt to characterize this being in crude and stammering terms.

What can we find in ordinary, everyday Western culture that is analogous to the higher human being in the East? It takes a good deal of thought to discover the corresponding element that sets the tone for all of Western culture. Ordinary reference books tell us that there are approximately 1.5 billion people living on Earth. This is true enough if we count only the two-legged beings actively involved in the work of producing human culture, but it is not true in terms of how many people it would take to do this work, if it were performed *only* by humans, as was the case not too long ago. Increasingly, over the last three to four centuries, the achievements of Western culture have allowed us to replace human work with machine work to a considerable extent, and the goods that serve our culture are now the products of machine work as well as human work. If machines did not exist, we would soon realize how many more people would have to live on earth to make up the difference. The number of people needed to perform the work now done by machines can be estimated in terms of coal consumption and the like. When I did these calculations, I concluded that in addition to the current world population of 1.5 billion, 700 to 750 million additional people would have to be working on earth, assuming an eight-hour work day. In other words, it is only partially correct to say that 1.5 billion humans populate the earth. It is also populated by many others, who do the work humans would otherwise have to do, but these others are not human. They are humanoid machines. The Eastern psyche is somewhat uncomfortable with the idea that 700 to 750 million humanoids have invaded human culture.

These humanoid coworkers, these substitutes for human energy, are the typical Western analog or counterpart of the higher, spiritual human being in Eastern culture. I believe that the balance sheet of world culture would be incomplete if it did not include these two entries—the higher human being on the one hand and the subhuman on the other.

In recent times, of course, the peoples of Asia have not remained idealists, but have acquired the products of Western machinery for themselves. Nonetheless, let me cite an example from the mid-1870s, because it is still characteristic of the overall structure of the spiritual culture of the East. At that time, the Japanese received their first steam-operated warships from the English. Proud to have these ships at their command, they sent their English instructors off with thanks and set out themselves. People watched from the shore as one captain turned a ship under full steam, but they grew somewhat uncomfortable as the ship went on turning and turning and wouldn't stop turning. The Englishman who knew how to control the steering mechanism had been sent away, and so the Japanese captain had to keep turning and turning out there on the open ocean until the steam ran out. Of course such national differences are no longer so apparent in practical matters, but they are still evident to a considerable extent to our respective inner constitutions. The relationship of educated Asians to Western intellectual culture is essentially still that of the Japanese captain who did not know how to turn off the steam. There are tremendous differences in Eastern and Western cultures—in effect, an abyss still to be bridged. It is very difficult for members of one culture to find their way into the other with full inner honesty.

That is why we in Central Europe, wedged in between the cultures of East and West, now find ourselves in difficulty. Only the last remnants of Eastern spiritual culture suggest what that culture once was. Inasmuch as we belong to the Western world, we in central Europe were nourished by Eastern culture for a long time. Although the event of Golgotha happened in the Middle East, it took place to benefit all of humankind and therefore cannot be said to have come from Eastern spiritual culture. Everything that allowed the Western hearts and minds to understand the Mystery of Golgotha, however, did indeed come from (Middle) Eastern traditions. To an unbiased view, our Christian way of thinking about this event is the last outcome of Eastern influence.

Today our normal, everyday culture still survives on influxes from Asia and has not yet produced any new approaches to understanding the Mystery of Golgotha and other supersensible events. But now that Eastern spiritual culture is in decline, although still adapted to modern Asians, what has it become in Europe and in Europe's extension in America? All the last vestiges of ancient Eastern spiritual currents that allowed us to understand the supersensible have become empty phrases. If we are truly aware of our modern life of soul and intellect, we must realize that a great deal of its content has been replaced by empty phrases. We are still thinking using words either directly derived from, or modeled after, ancient Eastern usage, but these words—and with them, a large part of our mental activity— have become devoid of meaning. Words that once held great significance in the ancient spiritual culture of the East have become empty in our mouths, in our understanding, and in our hearts.

Unfortunately for our time, we are not yet sufficiently aware of this emptiness. Empty phrases that suffice for formulating party programs and clichéd worldviews can never give rise to fruitful actions or ideas to further humankind's development. Empty phrases can incite and propagandize, but they cannot create. Looking at the legacy of Eastern spiritual culture, we realize that the living spiritual world it once held has become empty phrases. Then we turn to the mechanistic element that has become essential to Western culture. How do we perceive this element when the resilience of a spiritual culture no longer supports our perception? Can we deny that we take it for granted that mechanical energy replaces 700 to 750 million people on Earth, or that this fact dominates our social and political thinking and has invaded our heads?

Admittedly, our culture contains a few exceptions. There have been Western individuals who sensed such things on a deeper level. Let me draw your attention once again to an important creative work by the Austrian poet Robert Hamerling, namely, his "Homunculus."[†] In this epic poem, published in the 1880s, Hamerling attempts to portray the peculiarly egotistical aspirations of a man who is entirely the product of our mechanistic culture. This man is portrayed as a billionaire, whose soul is driven out by mechanistic thinking. Hamerling also anticipates many innovations (such as air traffic) that had not yet become realities in his time. To Hamerling, the soul-spiritual life of a typical member of Western civilization is that of a homunculus—an artificial, machine-like human being shaped by the mechanistic powers of the outer world rather than by internalized manifestations of the supersensible world.

When we consider keenly perceptive descriptions of Western life by a modern educated man of the East, such as Tagore, we experience secondhand the fervor of the author's spiritual worldview as he reclaims the spiritual world of the East. Although Tagore speaks in Eastern nuances I cannot imitate, he describes all of the Western world's perceptions of nature and social or political thinking in the same way as Hamerling's homunculus. In Western culture, the echoes of the former spiritual greatness of the East have become mere empty phrases; to Asians, the great achievements of Western civilization are humanoid culture.

People who take the easy way out will accuse me of exaggerating, I know, but only because they lack the courage to call a spade a spade, or resist understanding. In spite of their objections, it is time for an honest accounting in our collective soul-spiritual life. We must be especially aware of the liabilities of Western culture that I have described here today. The aftermath of the last world catastrophe should finally make it tangibly obvious—as was evident to any unbiased view even before 1914—that the humanoid character of the Anglo-American empire has spread over much of the world.

I am not saying this because I happen to be speaking in a German city. I have made similar statements elsewhere in recent weeks, and for quite some time now, I have also been telling Anglo-Americans that Central Europeans are actually better off than they are, because a great deal of responsibility has now shifted from the German-speaking nations to the Anglo-American side. We have it easier because we no longer bear such responsibility for "the rapacious acquisition of foreign territory," as one perceptive Englishman recently described it to me. By contrast, anyone who lives in an Anglo-American nation and still has some human sensitivity must feel the burden of a gigantic responsibility for humankind's further development.

For us, however, what is the crucial aspect of the mechanistic international culture epitomized by the Anglo-American world? As a representative of spiritual science, I am not about to issue a thunderous, reactionary denunciation of this mechanistic culture, nor would it occur to me even for a moment to express any backward-looking thoughts about restoring old institutions or doing away with even a single achievement of our modern culture. We must respect the inevitabilities of the world's evolution, and modern mechanistic culture is as necessary and inevitable as the old spiritual culture. But what is its crucial element? Eastern culture, before it fell into decadence, focused on striving for the divine spirit in each individual. Today, however, this culture has become the product of martyr-like drives and has largely exchanged its spiritually-based management of public affairs for a version imported from Western Europe. The East has lost its greatness and its inner impulse, and the breath of the past hangs over its spiritual culture. The fact that many Westerners are now turning to the East for help with their own faltering spiritual life is also a sign of decadence—a sign that all good spirits have been forced out of Western humanity. The current outer manifestations of Eastern culture, however, have no future. Grotesque as it may sound, the breath of the future hangs over our Western mechanistic culture.

I am not speaking as a reactionary when I talk about Western culture, nor do I want to do away even its smallest detail. Nonetheless, it remains a fact that as this culture spread through the labor of its 700 to 750 million subhuman, mechanized inhabitants, we real humans were left no life of spirit and soul capable of energetically intervening in such a mechanized world. It is my belief—or rather, it is an insight derived from spiritual science, which is more than just a belief—that the same spiritual energy that, when applied exclusively to the sense-perceptible world of space and time, manifests in mechanics and great technology also inspires anthroposophical spiritual science as I have presented it over the last two decades. The spiritual activity that created our machines and our mechanistic culture would have been impossible to reconcile with the spiritual life of the creators of Eastern spiritual culture. Such spiritual activity would have crushed them. They were not meant to be surrounded by mechanized life, but we Westerners are. We are meant to apply our intelligence and employ all of our human forces of spirit and soul in developing the inner strength to master our mechanized electro-technical culture in its entirety.

Starting from the same basic spiritual configuration, we must transcend the sense-perceptible world to develop the soul-forces that I described in *How to Know Higher Worlds* and the second part of *The Philosophy of Freedom*. These soul forces will lead us into supersensible worlds in a way that was never possible in the ancient East. Taking as our starting point the same spirit that suffuses the laws governing our machinery and electronics, we must undergo inner development that allows us to perceive the spiritual worlds that Easterners once saw, but we must perceive them in a different way—a way that is as rigorously scientific as the methods of any modern science. We Westerners, however, are at the very beginning of this process, and as yet very few people acknowledge that it is possible, let alone necessary. Nonetheless, we must develop a spiritual science that is equal in power and comprehension to all of the scientific and cognitive efforts known in the modern Western world. As we attempt to characterize this new, spiritual science, we cannot resort to mouthing the empty phrases that are becoming the currency of religious denominations. The same seriousness and drive that we apply to our outer sciences must also be applied to developing spiritual science.

We have now seen the outcome of a rational effort to add up the assets and liabilities of our time. If we continue to develop our social and political views only on the basis of the natural sciences, then we will post only liabilities; and our sociological or historical overviews will explain only the dying aspects of our public and historical affairs. The natural sciences allow us to understand only dead matter, and if we apply the science of death to public and historical activity, we will understand only their dying aspects. This explains why new social theories, which are now actually being implemented after a period of merely criticizing the status quo, are having such deadly effects on real life: they were created in the image of death. We will derive truly socially responsible views only from sources that must also feed our modern supersensible activity. Viewpoints derived from a merely mechanistic view of nature are liabilities, as are lifeless copies of centuries-old religious denominations that have lost their vitality. Now, more than at any other time, humankind needs the power of the Christ, but we need a new way to find him. All of the old ways, whether obvious or disguised, belong in the liability column. We need assets, and in this case the assets will come from the renewal of our spiritual worldview. Today this path is still too difficult for many, especially in the West. Lately we have seen the emergence of an odd quasi-spiritual trend. Instead of learning about the spiritual world through the human soul's own strengths, it attempts to do so through imitations of scientific experiments that entice gods or spirits or the souls of the dead to pay the occasional visit to the physical, sense-perceptible world. Spiritism makes do with such theatrical displays, but they are the opposite of a genuine quest for spirit. If we truly seek spirit today, it is not enough to receive the occasional visit from spiritual beings on display in a theater in order to prove the existence of a spiritual world that we ignore in our outer life. We cannot allow the materialistic course of our life to continue. What have scientists like Lombroso done?† The natural sciences remain devoid of spirit for them, so scientists turn to spiritualism to discover something beyond the natural world. Meanwhile the rest of their lives becomes ever more materialistic. What we really need, however, is spiritual deepening that can truly make inroads into our material life and accompany it every step of the way.

My ongoing mission is to describe a spiritual view of life complete with ideas that can shape actions and soul-forces that can generate morality and religious reverence. I will continue to demonstrate that this spiritual science is already here in the content of my lectures over the past two decades. Today my intention was to describe this spiritual striving as an asset to offset the many liabilities of our modern culture. No matter what the political future holds, it should be possible for the much-tested German-speaking peoples, wedged in between East and West as we are, to base a new quest for spirit on the groundwork done by our great cultural forebears. In future, if we have the inner energy to take this route to the spirit, we should be able to tell the East about a spiritual life that it once possessed, in different form, but has since lost. The East will receive this from us if we succeed in informing the West about spiritual activity that can meet all the challenges presented by our purely mechanistic culture. If we seek this new route to the spirit, we will fulfill an essential task in Central Europe.

The recent catastrophic events seem to have held strange consequences for the German-speaking peoples. It is quite true that we not only allowed ourselves to be overwhelmed by the precipitous ascendancy of economic activity in the West but we also took part in the search for spiritual renewal in the impotent East. Nonetheless, it seems to me—I will resist the temptation to say "it is a fact"—that even at the peak of our materialistic aspirations, we proved we have no gift for materialism. We must look elsewhere for that gift, in some other part of the world. If adversity leads us to recognize our lack of talent for materialism, perhaps this recognition will encourage us to explore a spirituality that is our own, and not borrowed from the East. Perhaps the roots of our strength, which lie in the pure distillation of thinking, to which German culture aspired at the turn of the eighteenth to the nineteenth century, will still give rise to spiritual work on behalf of the further development of humanity as a whole. Whatever else the fate of the German people may entail, if we seek spiritual renewal by returning to our cultural roots, we will realize that the Germanic spirit has not yet reached its peak.† It will live on in future actions and future concerns, and we hope it will still inform humanity's future from this spiritual perspective.

# 6

## Spirit Cognition as a Basis for Action

STUTTGART, DECEMBER 30, 1919

ABOUT two years ago, as the catastrophic events of recent years were drawing to a close, the friends of the college of spiritual science in Dornach decided to rename its building.† You will immediately sense the significance of the new name: the Goetheanum. It expresses an awareness of German culture that will inspire us with the courage to confront any present and future challenges to that culture. And so the Goetheanum stands on a hill in northwest Switzerland as an emblem of a spirit that is truly international, and yet includes the significant element we associate with the name Goethe. With that reasoning in mind, perhaps I may be allowed to remind you of Goethe's thinking now and then in my lectures. I will begin today with an example that initially appears far-fetched, but in fact points to a characteristic aspect of our spiritual science.

You may recall that Goethe undertook an exhaustive study of plants and animals after assuming his responsibilities in Weimar. In the mid 1780s, after years of observation and experimentation in Weimar and Jena, he traveled to Italy, where his ideas on the relationship between plants and the earth coalesced. In letters to friends at home in Weimar, he wrote that he was very close to fully understanding the archetypal plant, the motif—perceptible only in spirit—that unites and underlies all individual plant forms. In a noteworthy passage, he wrote that once having grasped this "sensible-supersensible" figure, as he called it, we could then modify it to invent an infinite array of imaginary plants possessing all the inherent logic and necessity of plants that actually exist out there in meadows and woods and on mountainsides.[†]

When he wrote these words, Goethe sensed that his perception in this particular field of knowledge was approaching its peak. His statement tells us that he was attempting to develop a "spiritually appropriate" (as he put it) way of perceiving the natural world—a means of acquiring knowledge, which engages not only the senses and human intelligence, but also the entire spiritual aspect of the human being. This type of cognition submerges itself in the essence of living things, becoming one with them to such an extent that the creative energy manifesting in plant growth in the outer world and the living energy at work in creating the corresponding "ideas" in the human soul are experienced as being one and the same.

Goethe was clearly aware of the growth-force active in plants as they develop leaf-by- leaf, node-by-node, flower-by-flower. He wanted to connect with that creative force, to allow it to live in his own soul. His intention was to allow the forces inherent in outer objects to come alive in his conceptions of them.

This approach to knowledge aspires to an extremely intimate sharing of experience with outer living things. By now, our cognitive processes are very different, so we underestimate how greatly Goethe's effort to achieve living ideas has impacted humanity's striving for knowledge. Our spiritual science, however, intends to be "Goethean" —not in the sense of compiling anthologies of what Goethe said or wrote on scientific subjects, but by taking up and developing Goethe's initial, elementary efforts so that they may become increasingly fruitful. The spirit that worked in Goethe continued to grow and develop even after he was dead to this world, and the possibilities for its further unfolding are very different now than they were at the time of his death in 1832. Goetheanism in 1919 does not need to rehash Goethe's literal words, but it must continue to work in the same spirit. This can best be done by expanding Goethe's efforts—which were limited to the field of botany and, to a lesser extent, zoology—into the impulse behind a comprehensive worldview that, above all else, includes the human being. This new Goetheanism will transform the worldview that is emerging from our culture's most respected (that is, scientific) methods of acquiring knowledge.

Let me refer back to earlier lectures and characterize civilized humanity's spiritual evolution over the last four centuries. During this period, intellectual, rational thinking emerged as the primary force in our collective development and our striving for knowledge. As the natural sciences experienced major triumphs and provided an abundance of scientific information on outer realities, our way of relating to the outer world—that is, the inner process of shaping ideas about the natural world and about our life— became thoroughly intellectual.

It is true that we enter a highly spiritual element when we allow ourselves to be guided primarily by the intellectual aspect of human nature. The abstract ideas and concepts we have cultivated over the last four centuries are inherently spiritual, but they are incapable of becoming anything more than reflections of outer, sense-perceptible realities. The most characteristic element of modern soul-spiritual life is its gradual development of abstract, very finely differentiated ideas and concepts, which lack the inherent energy needed to approach anything beyond sense-perceptible reality. People who apply great mental effort to this intellectual approach often believe themselves to be totally free of any bias or presupposition in pursuing their lines of thinking or research. This activity, however, is by no means independent of historical developments. It is interesting to note that many self-designated philosophers or scientists believe that human nature, or the nature of the world itself, determine or require one or the other method of research, when in fact their methods are simply the outcome of a thousand years of human conditioning.

Since the fifteenth century, we in the Western civilized world have been entirely devoted to intellectual thinking. We find its prelude in the last few centuries before Christ, in the dialectics of ancient Greece. Dialectics involves the inner activation of an element of thought that leads to increasing abstraction. To an unbiased view of Greek life, this process (which was still very much imbued with spirit for Plato, but became mere logical activity for Aristotle) is clearly derived from an even older, completely soul-filled thinking. If we look back to the earliest period in the development of Greek thinking and culture—as Nietzsche did in a grandiose if somewhat pathological way, calling it the "tragic age" of Greece—we discover that the abstract, dialectical, logical element is not yet present, nor is the exclusive focus on the outer world. That early stage of Greek culture still contained an element that can arise only out of innermost human nature, which presents, in a great diversity of manifestations, the essence of the world as if from within.

If we look still further back in time for the origins of the intellectual logic that first began to appear in Greece, we find in the East a type of mystery-cognition that is, in fact, mysterious only to modern humanity. Today, in our ordinary life, we no longer have any conception of this means of acquiring knowledge. In the schools of the ancient East that served simultaneously as art institutes and religious centers, individuals did not merely learn or apply their intellectual abilities to research. In the Eastern mystery centers, it went without saying that people embedded in ordinary life could not follow the path to the mysteries of existence. Before being allowed to approach these mysteries, students had to completely transform their inner constitution through rigorous inner self-discipline. They had to transform themselves into different beings fit to receive mystery knowledge. The ancient East cultivated a means of cognition based on rich, concrete soul-spiritual activity. This fact cannot be documented historically, but it can be confirmed by spiritual science. Eastern mystery activity spread to Europe, where it became increasingly filtered down into dialectics, logic, and mere intelligence in ancient Greece, and later (beginning around the middle of the fifteenth century) into the intellectualism of modern civilization.

Without a complete inner view of these facts, we cannot make sense of the various currents in modern culture or their assets and liabilities, nor can we achieve fruitful perceptions of modern humanity's needs. It is time to take an uncompromising look at our spiritual history and recognize the spiritual worlds in which we are embedded. Having traced the line of development from the "imported" spiritual life of the East through Greece and into our modern intellectualism, we must now look at *how* this evolution occurred. It was possible only because it was linked to a natural facet of the human constitution: namely, heredity or blood relationships. We must base any study of the evolution of human cognition on insight into the full scope of the influence of blood relationships. In the ancient times that produced the precursors of our modern cognitive processes, perception and knowledge were bound to heredity and appeared in different forms in different races, ethnic groups, and other groups of people related by blood. The esoteric training of students admitted to the mystery schools had to be adapted to their bloodlines and inherited gifts and temperaments, which provided the natural basis for cultivating spiritual cognition.

If we are aware of the real evolutionary history of humankind (in contrast to the *fable convenue* we now call history), we will discover that in the Western civilized world, the ties binding human mental activity to blood ties were severed abruptly around the mid-1400s, when they began to be replaced by factors that can never be inherited. This change is apparent in all post-fourteenth century art, which has emerged from sources of human mental activity totally unrelated to even the greatest of the nature-based, elementally-tinged accomplishments of earlier times. The difference is evident in many artistic media. The ancient Greeks were still aware that the creative energy at work in their culture—in the work of Aeschylus, for example, or the philosophy of Heraclitus or Anaxagoras—was bound to the bloodlines of specific ethnic groups. We can confirm this relationship for ourselves by looking at artwork such as typical Greek sculptures, which reveal three distinct physical types: the satyr, the Mercury type (especially evident in all busts of Mercury), and the type common to sculptures of Zeus, Hera, Athena, and Apollo. If you look carefully at the shape of the nose, ears, and all the other details of each of these three types, it will become obvious that the Greeks viewed the satyr and Mercury types as inferior human bloodlines and depicted Zeus as an example of superior humanity. These differences express the Greeks' sense of connection between spirituality and the natural, elemental, inherited factor in human evolution. This connection gradually loosened until it ceased to mean anything at all to humankind around the middle of the fifteenth century, when the intellectual element began to predominate in all normal, outer manifestations of spirituality. Since that time, our mental activity is no longer bound to heredity or blood relationships. Today, even the pettiest philosophizers must admit that intellectual ideas no longer have anything to do with the fact of blood kinship, which played such a major role in ancient spirituality.

The highly attenuated, purely intellectual mental life that has evolved since the mid-1400s has taught us to become independent of the merely natural element, but it has also distanced us from everything once considered essential to being human. A unique and even tragic feature has entered humankind's evolution. We have risen to a level of experience that is independent of natural, elemental forces, but these experiences no longer allow us to understand ourselves. In ancient, blood-bound spirituality, inner insight naturally included knowledge of the essential nature of the human being. Now, however, we have risen to an abstract level of spirituality that experiences great scientific triumphs but is incapable of exploring human nature.

Looking back on the stage of mental evolution that was based on natural, elemental factors, we find that good or bad, sympathetic or antipathetic actions in human history were also expressions of blood-based means of experiencing spirit. Individuals experienced themselves and spirituality through their bloodline. Their blood supplied mighty images or imaginations of the spirit they experienced. These soul-experiences then flooded their bodies, and their ideas became deeds.

But what about today? After three or four hundred years, intellectual development has culminated, and the modern civilized world is full of the results of intense intellectual research. We find a great variety of ideas, but they have all become too abstract, too remote from life, to transform into impulses for action. Today, when humankind's social and other problems have become acute, our souls seem to have fallen into a collective sleep that does not allow us to acknowledge that we are sliding down a slippery slope. The need for more profound inner forces that can inspire action is becoming urgent. Instead, we hear abstract religious preaching that bears no relationship to real life, reminding us of the old folksong: "Sleep, Michael, sleep/ In the garden goes a sheep,/ in the garden goes a little priest,/ leading you to heaven. /Sleep, Michael , sleep!" We have lost any connection between perceiving the natural world outside us, which has become a purely intellectual process, and perceiving the essential nature of the human being, which was formerly a natural part of ancient, blood-based spiritual cognition.

I know how reluctant people have become to hear such seemingly outlandish, fantastical, and exaggerated descriptions. But if we are not willing to hear them, we will fail to develop fruitful ideas about how to renew and reorganize our life. To any unbiased view, such ideas are desperately needed. As for spirit and soul, although our academic philosophers still talk about the human "soul" in relationship to the outer world, any clear understanding of the human being as an entity of body, soul, and spirit has long since disappeared from our Western worldview. At this point we confront a very strange phenomenon. As I have said in many previous lectures, the triad of body, soul, and spirit is essential to understanding the true nature of the human being. The body serves as the spirit's instrument between birth and death; the soul is neither body nor spirit, but unites them both. Without a thorough grasp of this trinity, we cannot break through to a true understanding of the essence of human nature. Nowadays, however, even outstanding philosophers, who believe their scholarly efforts are unbiased, say that the human being consists of body and soul. They do not know that our intellectual activity is based on a long developmental history in the East. For example, in 869 A.D. the Eighth Ecumenical Council of Constantinople[†] decreed that, as Christians, we must believe that the human being consists, not of body, soul and spirit, but only of a body, and a soul with some spiritual attributes. From that time on, this statement became dogma in the Catholic Church and an underlying assumption in academic research. Today people who believe they are conducting independent research are really simply following the edict of the Eighth Ecumenical Council of 869, which abolished the human spirit by decree.

As a result of such influences, our mental activity has become so abstract and intellectual that it is no longer capable of engendering will impulses. In time, if our Western intellectual life becomes entirely materialistic, our ability to act will be completely paralyzed.

The course of Western intellectual development must teach us the need for a spiritual renewal of our culture. We have lost any blood-bound insight into higher human nature and must now regain it from a different perspective. It was both necessary and right for humanity to spend three or four centuries developing the independent intellect. We achieved a certain freedom from natural constraints, but the resulting intellectualism must now be re-imbued with soul and spirit—with knowledge that informs and inspires human actions. Anthroposophical spiritual science has nothing to do with reviving the ancient methods of the East. Instead, it aspires to a modern means of learning about spirit. Anthroposophy wants to achieve a degree of intimacy with the life of the universe, which allows us to recognize the growth forces of the natural and spiritual worlds in our own bodies, as well as in plants and animals. If we imbue our intellectual activity with experiences of spirit, independent (rather than blood-bound) spirit cognition will inspire and strengthen our actions.

Human will and human actions would be paralyzed without the influence of spirit perception. It is simplistic to say that anthroposophical spiritual science retreats into the contemplative life to achieve its knowledge. So does chemistry. Chemists acquire their knowledge in classrooms and laboratories that are entirely separate from the practical applications of chemistry. The contents of real spirit cognition, which can tell us about the true nature of the human being, must still be acquired through individual self-transformation, although now in a completely different way than in the ancient mysteries. It is now time for us to learn spirit cognition, just as we learn to perceive with our senses and to reason with our intellect. Two lectures ago, I talked about the need for intellectual modesty. It takes intellectual modesty to realize that, as human beings involved in outer life between birth and death, we are not naturally equipped to enter the spiritual world. Approaching the real mysteries of the natural and spiritual worlds requires learning, just as five-year-olds must learn how to read. To the extent that we make use of our physical bodies, we are not adapted to the world of spirit. Experiencing this limitation is painful. Achieving real insight into human nature involves renunciation and the willingness to undergo painful experiences, as should be obvious from the fact that anyone capable of perception in the spiritual world is no longer looking at the world with ordinary eyes, hearing with ordinary ears, or thinking in the ordinary way. Spirit cognition requires an independent spiritual organism. While it is certainly true that entering the spiritual world involves practices that isolate us from life's outer turmoil, the achievements of our spiritual science do not deserve to be described as an otherworldly mysticism that is remote from or hostile to life. Knowledge gained through spiritual research conducted in isolation can be understood with healthy common sense and can inspire and inform human intentions and actions.

By cultivating an all-embracing Goethean approach, anthroposophical spiritual science aspires to a form of spirit cognition that can serve as the foundation for energetic human action. That is the only way to help our world. Although intellectual knowledge is also acquired through inner effort, it applies at best only to technology, that is, to the non-human world. Impulses derived from spiritual knowledge, however, can guide our public life, which has grown so difficult, in the direction of true recovery. Perhaps these claims of spiritual science deserve greater consideration in view of the infinite human suffering caused by failed so-called social movements such as Leninism, Trotskyism, and the like, which are nothing more than intellectual poison. For four hundred years, intellectualism helped to free human beings to be individuals, but it served this useful purpose only as long as it did not attack old social forms. As soon as pure intellectualism seeks to transform society, its horrendous toxic effects become increasingly evident. It is a terrible illusion to believe that we can afford to look on world events dispassionately. These toxic effects are still in their early stages, and recovery can come only from spirit. Spirit cognition must become the basis of social renewal.

I wish our opponents would take an uncompromising look at what is actually happening in our life instead of issuing all kinds of (sometimes) well-meaning proclamations about how spiritual science should keep out of religion. For example, a Protestant clergyman,[†] who gave a lecture on anthroposophy here in Stuttgart, reportedly said that although spiritual science may unearth all sorts of clairvoyant forces, it has nothing to do with the childish simplicity that a Christian view of religion requires. Only someone who has been abandoned by all the spirits responsible for humankind's evolution could utter such a statement. To those they have not abandoned, these spirits proclaim loudly and clearly that this abstract talk of uniting some indefinable something in the human being with the Christ, this misguided enthusiasm for the childlike element in religion, is what led to society's current woes in the first place. First the element of soul and spirit was monopolized by religious denominations, and the result was a science that is devoid of spirit and presents a spiritless image of the natural world. And now, although they admit that spiritual science can reveal all sorts of spiritual realities, they ask us to avow that these realities have nothing to do with the divine nature we are supposed to be seeking in ourselves. The materialism of the natural sciences has done a good job of eliminating spirit from nature, and this type of religiosity will increasingly eliminate God from spirit. In the end, we will be left with nature with no spirit, spirit with no God, and a religion with no content.

A religion without content, however, cannot inspire actions. Without spirit cognition our ethical impulses on behalf of Western culture are totally unfounded. Ethical impulses originate within and demand to be implemented in real life in a way that intellectual understanding does not, as a little unbiased self-observation will confirm. Ethical impulses or intuitions are very different from the intellectually formulated knowledge of modern science.

Our modern intellectualism, however, is unable to bridge the gap between our understanding of nature and our ethical activity. What has become of our ethical worldview as a result? Apart from religious views that are more or less devoid of content, the only other worldview available to us has been cobbled together on the basis of the natural sciences, and as such it is highly one-sided, although at least honest. According to this view, our world (complete with human beings and other living things) gradually developed out of a primordial mist through certain combinations of vortex phenomena. But what about human ethical ideals and intuitions? If we believe in natural combinations as the sole origin of all things, ethical intuitions are mere epiphenomena that are valid only as long as people think they are. If the many old instincts remaining from earlier stages of human mental evolution were eliminated from our inner life and not replaced, we would have to resort to outer confirmation of our ethical ideals. Instead of feeling that we owe our ideals to the spiritual life that transcends all physical life, our motivation for action would simply be the desire to appear respectable in other people's eyes, or to avoid breaking the law. In short, if the intellect remains dominant, we will lose any sense that our ethical activity is warmed and enthused by a soul-spiritual element. Ethical activity will be a reality only when spirit perception suffuses all of the mental processes we have acquired over the past three to four hundred years.

These remarks are not intended as reactionary criticism; they are simply meant to point out a real need. But what does spirit perception reveal, and what does it have to do with ethics? In the entire natural world, spirit perception sees the beginnings of what reasonable geologists—I use the term "reasonable" here in a relative sense—consider true of geological formations. These geologists say that a large part of the Earth's surface is already in a state of decline, which means we are walking around on a dead entity. The presence of dead substance, however, is not limited to geology. Our culture is full of it, and recent science has focused exclusively on the non-living aspects of the natural world. We are gradually becoming surrounded by elements that date back to primeval stages of evolution and are in their final stage of existence in the Earth phase of evolution. In contrast to these dying elements, our ethical ideals and intuitions (as revealed to anthroposophical spiritual science) are like the germ of the next plant that is already present in a dying flower, whereas the dying flower itself is the legacy of the earlier plant. In the natural world, we experience the dying legacy of earlier evolutionary phases; in the ethical ideals that come to life within us, we experience an element that will accompany human souls out into cosmic, eternal life when the Earth is cast off like so much slag or like a collective corpse. By cultivating our ethical activity, we sow the seeds of future metamorphoses of the Earth.

Of course, this idea still seems preposterous to most modern human beings. But, if we take it completely seriously and are fully aware of its depth, just imagine the impact it could have on our sense of moral responsibility! As human beings, we are products of the past, including all of the Earth's evolution, and as such we are on the road to decline. The ethical impulses alive in us, however, are the seeds of a future that still seems unreal and abstract, but in fact these impulses are the earliest beginnings of an abundant reality to come. We must realize that if we fail to cultivate ethical activity, we transgress not only against our fellow human beings, but also against all of the spiritual worlds that have planted the seeds of the future in us in the form of ethical impulses. If you behave unethically, you are cut off from humanity's future. In addition to infusing our will and actions with strength, spirit cognition also lends our ethical activity a cosmically-oriented sense of responsibility for our fellow human beings. In comparison, the thought-horizon of educated ancient Greeks feels very limited: they were citizens of their city-states. In more recent times, America was discovered and the fact that the Earth is round was rediscovered through direct experience. As a result, we became citizens of Earth. Now it is time to take the next step. Today we are called upon to become citizens of the cosmos in the truest sense, to feel not only that we belong to worlds that exist outside of our own yet form a whole with it, but also that we contribute to future worlds.

Through spirit cognition, our ethical views gain new roots. We will be able to transform ethics into an active force for social change only when spirit cognition lends strength to our ethical activity.

The methods I have suggested apply to the threefolding of the social organism as I describe it in *Toward Social Renewal*. The views expressed in that book are often held to be abstract or utopian, yet they are more realistic than any others. This is because they are based on a new understanding of reality that none of our natural sciences, infected as they are with intellectual thinking, can possibly achieve. The gradual development of intellectualism has thrown individuals back on themselves to an unprecedented extent. Today, we see strange examples of how egotistical people become when they can no longer understand the natural world and the human being on the same basis. Together with intellectualism, egotism has pervaded all of our outer and inner life in the last three to four centuries. It has become especially apparent in religion, as an unbiased view is forced to admit. These centuries have taught us to think about the immortality of the human soul from a peculiarly egotistical perspective. Today, individuals tremble in fear of the possibility that they might cease to exist as soul-spiritual beings when their dead bodies are laid to rest. (That is not what happens, of course, but people fear it nonetheless.) Dogma forces us to focus entirely on life after death (the existence of which spiritual science fully corroborates, of course) while ignoring our existence as soul-spiritual beings in a spiritual world before conception and birth. The truth of the matter, however, is that before descending into the physical body provided through heredity, each of us undergoes a period of development in a world of spirit and soul just as we do here on Earth. And just as life after death is a continuation of earthly life and builds on its experiences, the life we lead between birth and death is a continuation of life before birth.

Being aware of life before birth arouses a totally different sense of responsibility, especially in teachers. It is no small matter to educate beings, who descend from eternal spiritual heights into human bodies, which they then shape to their own purposes more precisely with each passing year. Life before birth is the other half of the picture, the complement to the human soul's immortality after death, which we accept as a matter of course because it gratifies our egotistical desires. That is why spiritual science places so much emphasis on the fact that life here on Earth is a continuation of the life we lived before birth or conception. Focusing exclusively on the afterlife makes it easy to avoid worldly responsibility. If we take life before birth equally seriously, we feel an obligation to lead an active and effective life on Earth. Exclusive focus on the afterlife leads to a physical existence devoid of soul and spirit, but awareness of a previous existence in spirit before we descended into physical, sense-perceptible existence strengthens our will and pervades all of our life's activities. Only spirit perception offers a sound basis for human hopes for the future. Imbuing our intellectual nature with the results of spiritual science will bring effective will impulses back into human life on Earth, which is now on the decline. Earlier generations could still rely on their instincts. In ancient Greece, for example, those who came of age and were ready to participate in public affairs simply needed to put their inherited instincts to use. Today that is no longer possible. All culture would disappear if we attempted to rely only on our earthly instincts, which is what the socialism of Eastern Europe does. In effect, it is relying on nothing. If we pin our hopes on a socialism based on spiritual science, however, we are relying on something real.

Of course, the perceptions and views I have presented here are not yet taken seriously by a large number of people, although some of our opponents take them seriously enough. For example, when I was still working in Dornach, I read in our magazine *Dreigliederung des sozialen Organismus* [Threefolding the Social organism] about a strange lecture given here in Stuttgart—complete with musical accompaniment, I believe—by a canon of the Catholic Church.[†] This lecture was based on systematic attacks by the Jesuit Father Otto Zimmerman, which have appeared in almost every issue of the Jesuit publication *Stimmen der Zeit* [Voices of the Time]. The lecturer said that Catholics wanting to inform themselves about what Steiner says should consult his opponents' writings, because the Pope has forbidden the reading of Steiner's own writings or those of his followers. The Roman Holy Congregation of July 18, 1919 issued a general edict forbidding the reading of theosophical and anthroposophical writings—at least according to Zimmermann's interpretation, and we cannot believe that the Jesuit Father always lies. That he does lie at times is evident from his assertion that I am a former priest, a deserter from a monastery, when in fact I never belonged to any monastery.[†] Later he retracted this statement, saying it can no longer be substantiated—a strange way to correct a lie! I do not, however, believe that he is lying about the edict forbidding Catholics to read my books. Clearly, these opponents of ours have some inkling of the fact that anthroposophical spiritual science is attempting to introduce very real forces into modern life.

In conclusion, let me make a comment that is both objective and personal. In the face of all resistance and to the best of its ability, anthroposophical spiritual science must continue to stand for knowledge that supports our actions, our ethical and social endeavors, and the finest human hopes. Our opponents may succeed in muzzling spiritual science, but as soon as it regains even the slightest freedom, it will resume speaking out about the truth it recognizes as necessary for humanity. When the tide began turning in favor of the Allies, the Goetheanum was there for the whole world to see, as testimony to an international culture unapologetically based on further development of a Goethean approach rooted in Germanic culture. Similarly, in spite of all obstacles, anthroposophical spiritual science will continue to fight for the perceptions and knowledge that shape its convictions. This content, although rooted in Central Europe, belongs to the whole world.

Thirty-five years ago, in my first attempt to describe what the Germanic character needs in order to regain its best spiritual sources of strength, I wrote these words as an exhortation to the German people: "In spite of all the progress we note in various fields of cultural activity, we cannot deny that the signature of our times leaves much to be desired. For the most part, our progress has been character-ized by breadth rather than depth, whereas an era's gains are judged entirely on the basis of their depth. Perhaps the proliferation of events that threaten to overwhelm us will make us understand that at the moment we have forfeited depth of vision for the sake of breadth. We can only hope that the frayed threads of progressive development will soon be joined together again and that we will be able to grasp new realities on the basis of the spiritual heights we once achieved."[†]

Thirty-five years ago, I sensed that a catastrophe was bound to occur if no legitimate spiritual resurgence developed to counteract this all-time cultural low. This feeling gnawed at my heart as I wrote these words and sent them to press. The course of events over the last three-and-a-half decades vindicates my decision to sound the call for spirituality. May this call not go unheard again! May the German people hear it now and in the near future; may they turn to spirituality to undo the terrible damage of recent years. In fact, the destruction is only beginning and will certainly continue unless we turn to the spirit in our efforts to rebuild our society and culture.

Today, let us appeal to the German people's will to cultivate spiri-tuality. We are quite justified in issuing this appeal, because there can be no doubt that we will find spirituality if we simply look for it. As I said recently, the events of the last few decades suggest that the

German people have no talent for materialism, whereas the spirit of centuries of German cultural development confirms our talent for spirituality. The call to spirituality must evoke a sense of great responsibility in us. May we become conscious of this responsibility in a way that allows us to contribute to humanity's evolution again by acting on our spiritual impulses. May we sustain, maintain and augment the accomplishments our greatest minds bestowed on a fortunate humanity for many centuries.

# REFERENCE NOTES

**Page 1, "*Towards Social Renewal*"**
(CW 23) *Towards Social Renewal: Rethinking the Basis of Society*, translated by
Matthew Barton, (London: Rudolf Steiner Press, 1999). First published in
English as *The Threefold Commonwealth* (London: Anthroposophical Publishing
Co., 1923). The second edition was titled *The Threefold Social Order* (New
York: Anthroposophic Press, 1966).

**Page 4, "He then wrote a book about his experiences."**
Alfred Kolb, *Als Arbeiter in Amerika*, 2nd ed., Berlin, 1904.

**Page 6, "a very important scientist"**
Emil Du Bois-Reymond (1818-1896), the father of experimental electrophysiol-
ogy. *Reden* ["Speeches"], 2 vol., Leipzig 1985-1887, 2nd ed. Leipzig, 1912.

**Page 6, "a scholarly society at the vanguard of German intellectual life"**
The Prussian Academy of Sciences, founded by Leibniz in 1700 at the encour-
agement of Friedrich I.

**Page 6, "one of the Hohenzollerns..."**
Friedrich Wilhelm I, who appointed the drunkard Gundling as President of the
Academy of Sciences to show his distain for academia.

**Page 7, "the scientific bodyguards of the Hohenzollerns"**
Rudolf Steiner paraphrases Du Bois-Reymond's statement, which read literally: "According to its deed of foundation, the University of Berlin, housed
across from the king's palace, is the intellectual bodyguard of the House of
Hohenzollern." From a speech as president of the University, August 3, 1870,
in *Reden*, vol. 1, 2nd ed., Leipzig, 1912, p. 418.

**Page 7, "founded by Liebknecht"**
See Chapter 28 of Rudolf Steiner's *Autobiography*, CW 28. Karl Liebknecht
(1871-1919), the son of Wilhelm Liebknecht, one of the founders of the Social
Democratic Party, was the co-founder in 1914 (with Rosa Luxemburg, among
others) of the Spartacist League and the Community Party of Germany (1919).
A revolutionary socialist, he died of a shot in the back of the head after torture
and interrogation in 1919.

**Page 8, "comprehensive schools are the only possible outcome..."**
A comprehensive school (Einheitschule) in this sense meant a school for all
social classes from the poorest to the richest. Thus Steiner will later speak of
the Waldorf School in Stuttgart as the first independent comprehensive school

because it served both the workers' children from Emil Molt's factory and the children of local Anthroposophists who came from all levels of society.

### Page 10, "Communist Manifesto"

The fundamental document of Socialism composed by Marx and Engles in pamphlet form and first published in 1848 in London.

### Page 12, "a certain number of years after the innovator's death"

Copyright for works of literature now expires seventy-five years after the death of the author.

### Page 13, "Aristotle said that capital should not produce offspring"

"The [Greek] word for 'interest' is roughly the same as 'offspring,' since money begets money and offspring tend to resemble their progenitors. Of all means of acquiring wealth, this is the most perverted." Aristotle, *Politics*, Book I, 1258b.

### Page 16, "at a small gathering in Vienna"

Rudolf Steiner refers here to his lecture to members of the Anthroposophical Society in Vienna on April 14, 1914, published in *Life Between Death and Rebirth* (CW 153) Literally, he said: "Today, therefore, production for market occurs without regard for consumption, rather than in the sense I presented in my essay 'Spiritual Science and the Social Question.' Everything that is produced is stockpiled in warehouses and through the money market, and then the manufacturers wait and see how much is purchased. This tendency is becoming ever more pronounced—to the point of self-destruction, as I am about to explain. The impact of production of this sort on the social organism is comparable to a cancer in the human body. From the spiritual perspective, we are looking at a horrible predisposition to cultural carcinoma. For anyone with a penetrating view of existence this terrible, oppressive prospect arouses great concern for our society. Even if we could suppress all of our enthusiasm for spiritual science— everything that makes us open our mouths and talk about it—this increasingly ominous prospect would still cause us to cry out for world healing."

### Page 16, "German Foreign Minister"

Gottlieb von Jagow, head of the German foreign service from 1913 to 1916.

### Page 17, "League of Nations conference"

March 7-13, 1919, in Bern. On March 11, Rudolf Steiner gave a public lecture in the Bern Council Hall, "A League of Nations' Real Basis in International Economic, Governmental, and Cultural Forces," in CW 329 (untranslated).

### Page 19, "theories of surplus value"

See Karl Marx, *Capital* [*Das Kapital*] (1867), and *Theories of Surplus Value*, 3 volumes (1862).

**Page 20, "Karl Marx himself said..."**
See the Friedrich Engels' letter to Conrad Schmidt, London, August 5, 1890: "The materialistic view of history also has a number of false friends today, which give it an excuse *not* to study history. Just as Marx said in reference to the French 'Marxists' of the last seventy years, all I know is that I am not a Marxist." Marx-Engels, Ausgewählte Briefe, Zürich 1934, Seite 371 f.

**Page 20, "events of 1870/71"**
The reference is to the Paris uprising and the institution of the celebrated anarchist-socialist Paris Commune following France's defeat in the Franco-Prussian War. Karl Marx, who witnessed the events, wrote about them extensively.

**Page 21, "the revolution of November 9 is over"**
There were three centers of "bloodless" revolution in November 1918: Kiel, Munich, and Berlin. November 9 refers to the Berlin "revolution," when, from the balcony of the Reichstag, socialists proclaimed Germany a Republic.

**Page 22, "The impulse of threefolding society was first presented..."**
See the Memoranda Rudolf Steiner sent to German and Austrian statesmen in July 1917, at the request of Counts Otto Lerchenfeld and Ludwig Polzer-Hoditz and reproduced in *Aufsätze über die Dreigliederung*, pp. 339 ff. A brief account is given in Henry Barnes, *A Life for the Spirit* (Hudson, NY: Anthroposophic Press, 1997).

**Page 22, "treaty of Brest-Litovsk"**
On March 13, 1918, the Soviet delegation signed the peace treaty under protest at the headquarters of the Eastern High Command. Russia relinquished Courland, Livonia, Estonia, Lithuania, and Poland; conceded to German troops the right to occupy Belarus until the signing of an international peace accord; pulled its troops out of Finland and the Ukraine; agreed to return to Turkey the Armenian territory conquered in 1878; and committed to paying reparations of six billion gold marks. The Treaty of Versailles annulled the Treaty of Brest-Litovsk.

**Page 22, "A brochure about responsibility for the war..."**
The brochure, published by the *Bund für Dreigliederung des sozialen Organismus*, contained recollections of the events of July-November 1914 by General Chief of Staff Helmuth von Moltke. With the agreement of Mrs. Eliza von Moltke, it also included an introduction by Rudolf Steiner. The brochure was never circulated. This material, without Steiner's introduction, did not appear until three years later in Moltke's collection of letters and documents covering the years 1877-1916. See also Steiner's *Essays on Threefolding*, op. cit., pp 386 ff.

**Page 22, "July 26"**
Two days before the Declaration of War on Serbia, the Austro-Hungarian ultimatum was made public.

**Page 33, "whether or not railroads should be built"**
See R. Hagen, *Die Erste Deutsche Eisenbahn* (1885), p. 45.

**Page 34, "the following example from scientific literature"**
See Louis Waldstein, "Das unterbewußte Ich und sein Verhältnis zu Gesundheit und Erziehung," Wiesbaden, 1908. See also Rudolf Steiner, "Das Ewige in der Menschenseele. Unsterblichkeit und Freiheit," GA 67, Dornach, 1962, pp. 291 ff.

**Page 37, "*The Education of the Child*"**
Rudolf Steiner, *The Education of the Child*, (Great Barrington, MA: Anthroposophic Press, 1996).

**Page 39, "Woodrow Wilson"**
Woodrow Wilson, 1856-1924, professor of law and political science at Princeton University and president of the United States, 1913-1921. He led the United States to war against the German Reich in 1917, shortly after being re-elected on a peace platform. In the last of his Fourteen Points of January 8, 1918, he proposed the establishment of a League of Nations. A joint English-American draft of its constitution was accepted at the Paris Peace Conference of 1919 and incorporated into individual peace treaties at Wilson's urging. Germany's request for immediate membership (alongside the victorious powers) was denied.

**Page 45, "in Vienna"**
See relevant note for page 16.

**Page 45, "foreign minister"**
See relevant note for page 16.

**Page 49, "Wilhelm Liebknecht"**
See relevant note for page 7.

**Page 49, "Walther Rathenau"**
Walther Rathenau, 1867-1922, German industrialist, politician, writer, and statesman who served as Foreign Minister of Germany during the Weimar Republic. He was assassinated by right-wing extremists.

**Page 52, "a scientist"**
See relevant notes for pages 6 and 7 on Emil Du Bois-Reymond.

**Page 52, "independent comprehensive school"**
The Independant Waldorf School opened its doors in Stuttgart on September 7, 1919. It was started by Rudolf Steiner at the invitation of Emil Molt (1876-1936), the president of the Waldorf-Astoria cigarette factory in Stuttgart.

**Page 52, "preparatory course for the faculty of the Waldorf School in Stuttgart"**
*The Foundations of Human Experience* (Great Barrington, MA: Anthroposophic Press, 1996) (also known as *Study of Man*) (CW 293), *Practical Advice to Teachers* (Great Barrington, MA: Anthroposophic Press, 2000) (CW 294), and *Discussions with Teachers* (Great Barrington, MA: Anthroposophic Press, 1997) (CW 295).

**Page 55, "Friedrich Engels"**
*Socialism: Utopian and Scientific*, written in 1880.

**Page 56, "Karl Marx said that a humanly unworthy existence..."**
Karl Marx, *Das Kapital*, vol. 1, section 3, chapter 4.3, "The Sale and Purchase of Labor."

**Page 58, "planned economy proposed by Moellendorff"**
Richard von Moellendorff (1881-1937), professor at the Technical University in Hannover and undersecretary in the Department of Trade and Industry in 1919, developed a plan for a federal socialized economy, but it was rejected by the National Assembly.

**Page 61, "We are like Faust saying to sixteen-year-old Gretchen"**
*Faust* Part One, 3438 ff.

**Page 64, "It has resounded in many hearts for over a century..."**
Schiller's *Don Carlos*: Act 3, Scene 10.

**Page 67, "(to use Goethe's words)"**
Goethe speaks of spirit eyes and spirit ears in many different contexts, for example, in *Dichtung und Wahrheit* ("Poetry and Truth"), Part 3, Book 11: "Not with the eyes of the body but with eyes of spirit, I saw myself approaching on horseback along the same path"; in *Naturwissenschaftliche Schriften, Zur Zoologie* ("Natural Scientific Works: On Zoology"): "We learn to see with eyes of spirit, without which we feel our way blindly, especially in natural science"; and in *Faust II*, Act 1, 4667 f.:

> The new day is a-borning,
> To spirit ears resounding.

**Page 68, "architectural ideas..."**
See Rudolf Steiner, *Architecture as a Synthesis of the Arts* (London: Rudolf Steiner Press, 1999) (CW 286).

**Page 72, "Woodrow Wilson..."**
See note for page 39.

**Page 72, "Wilson's book"**
*The New Freedom*, written in 1913.

**Page 78, "book by the Austrian statesman Czernin"**
Ottokar Czernin (1872-1932), Austrian Foreign Minister 1916-1918. *In the World War*. Book available online at www.gutenberg.org/etext/18160.

**Page 80, "the thoughts of a Japanese diplomat"**
To date, the Japanese diplomat has not been identified.

**Page 80, "recently published a brochure"**
Friedrich Traub, *Rudolf Steiner als Philosoph und Theosoph*, Tübingen, 1919, p. 34.

**Page 81, "an essay on Schiller and Goethe"**
Hermann Grimm, "Fünfzehn Essays. Erste Folge," Berlin, 1884, p. 116.

**Page 82, "Johann Gottlieb Fichte said something to this effect..."**
From Johann Gottlieb Fichte's preface to "Some Lectures Concerning the Scholar's Vocation." Available in: Trans. Daniel Breazeale. In *Fichte: Early Philosophical Writings*, pp. 144-184. [Complete translation of *Einige Vorlesungen Über die Bestimmung des Gelehrten* (1794). GA I, 3, pp. 25-68. SW, VI, pp. 289-346.]

**Page 83, "The young Nietzsche...declared..."**
Literally, "But of all the deleterious consequences of the recently fought war with France, the worst is perhaps one widely held, even universal error: the erroneous idea harbored by public opinion and all public opinionators that in this struggle German culture also came away victorious, and that it must therefore now be adorned with laurels befitting such extraordinary events and accomplishments. This delusion is extremely pernicious; not simply because it is a delusion—for delusions can be of a most salutary and blessed nature—but rather because it is capable of transforming our victory into a total defeat: into the defeat—indeed, the extirpation—of the German spirit for the sake of the 'German Reich'." This is the published translation from: *The Complete Works of Friedrich Nietzsche, Volume 2: Unfashionable Observations*. Translated by Richard T. Gray, Stanford University Press, 1995. First Piece: "David Strauss the Confessor and the Writer," p. 5.

**Page 84, "Strauss, *The Old Faith and the New*"**
*The Old Faith and the New*, written in Leipzig, 1872.

**Page 86, "Rabindranath Tagore"**
Rabindranath Tagore (1861-1941), author, philosopher, and freedom fighter

and the offspring of a Bengali family descended from the eighth-century Sanskrit playwright Bhatta-Narajana.

**Page 88, "Blavatsky and Besant"**
Helena Petrovna Blavatsky (1831-1891) co-founded the Theosophical Society with Henry Steel Olcott in 1875.
Annie Besant (1847-1933) was president of the Theosophical Society from 1907 until her death.

**Page 88, "the Theosophical Society branded us as heretics"**
See also Rudolf Steiner, *Autobiography* (CW 28), Chapter XXXI.

**Page 91, "an important creative work by the Austrian poet Robert Hamerling..."**
Robert Hamerling (1830-1889). His "Homunculus, A Modern Epic in 10 Cantos" was published in 1888. See also Rudolf Steiner's lecture, entitled "Homunculus," of March 26, 1914, in CW 63 and "Robert Hamerling: Poet, Thinker, and Human Being," a tribute compiled by Marie Steiner, Dornach, 1939.

**Page 95, "What have scientists like Lombroso done?"**
Cesare Lombroso (1836-1909), professor of forensic medicine and psychiatry in Turin, Italy, well-known for his theory about the connection between genius and insanity.

**Page 96, "The German spirit has not yet reached its peak"**
More literally, "The German spirit is not [yet] perfected." The latter wording is an aphorism Steiner gave at the end of his lecture in Berlin on January 14, 1915, "Die germanische Seele und der deutsche Geist vom Gisichtspunkte der Geisteswissenschaft," in CW 64, *Aus schicksaltragender Zeit* [Out of destiny-burdened times]. See also "Wahrspruchsworte" [Truth-wrought words], CW 40.

**Page 97, "decided to rename its building"**
The building in Dornach was originally called the *Johannesbau*, after one of the main figures in Rudolf Steiner's Mystery Dramas.

**Page 98, "noteworthy passage, he wrote..."**
See Goethe's letter to Herder of May 17, 1787, from *Italian Journey*. E.g., pp. 308-309 of the 1970 Penguin Classics edition.

**Page 103, "Eighth Ecumenical Council of Constantinople"**
Canon II of the *Canones contra Photium* stipulates that the human being does not have "two souls" but *unum animam rationabilem et intellectualem*. The

Council was called to condemn the Byzantine patriarch Photius, who upheld the need to distinguish between a lower and a higher, thinking human soul.

### Page 105, "For example, a protestant clergyman..."
The Protestant theologian Gogarten, later one of the leaders of the *Deutsche Christen* (the voice of Nazi ideology within the Evangelical Church), gave a series of lectures criticizing anthroposophy.

### Page 110, "a strange lecture given here in Stuttgart..."
In issue 21 of *Dreigliederung des sozialen Organismus*, Dr. Walter Johannes Stein reported on an adversarial lecture given in Stuttgart on November 11, 1919, by Canon Laun of Rothenburg: "The character of the speaker's weapons should be apparent from the fact that no discussion was allowed. He suggested that anyone wanting more information about Steiner consult a list of Steiner's opponents but not Steiner's own writings, which had been forbidden by the Pope."

### Page 110, "in fact I never belonged to any monastery"
*Stimmen aus Maria-Laach*, (retitled *Stimmen der Zeit* in 1914), Freiburg/Bremen 1912. On page 80 of volume 83 of this main publication of the Society of Jesus in Germany, Otto Zimmermann SJ discusses the book *Teosofia e Christianismo* by Giovanni Busnelli SJ. Zimmermann describes Rudolf Steiner as "an apostate priest, to judge by his behavior," while Busnelli speaks of him equally fallaciously as a "former Catholic priest." Not until six years later did Zimmermann retract his claim with the cursory phrase "which can no longer be substantiated." (*Stimmen der Zeit*, vol. 95,  p. 331)

### Page 111, "I wrote these words..."
"Die geistige Signatur der Gegenawart" in *Deutsche Wochenschrift*, 1888, vol. 6, no. 24. See CW 30, Dornach, 1961: *Methodische Grundlagen der Anthroposophie* [Methodical foundations of anthroposophy] 1884-1901, p. 253 ff.

# RUDOLF STEINER'S COLLECTED WORKS

The German Edition of Rudolf Steiner's Collected Works (the Gesamtausgabe [GA] published by Rudolf Steiner Verlag, Dornach, Switzerland) presently runs to over 354 titles, organized either by type of work (written or spoken), chronology, audience (public or other), or subject (education, art, etc.). For ease of comparison, the Collected Works in English [CW] follows the German organization exactly. A complete listing of the CWs follows with literal translations of the German titles. Other than in the case of the books published in his lifetime, titles were rarely given by Rudolf Steiner himself, and were often provided by the editors of the German editions. The titles in English are not necessarily the same as the German; and, indeed, over the past seventy-five years have frequently been different, with the same book sometimes appearing under different titles.

For ease of identification and to avoid confusion, we suggest that readers looking for a title should do so by CW number. Because the work of creating the Collected Works of Rudolf Steiner is an ongoing process, with new titles being published every year, we have not indicated in this listing which books are presently available. To find out what titles in the Collected Works are currently in print, please check our website at www.steinerbooks.org, or write to SteinerBooks 610 Main Street, Great Barrington, MA 01230:

## Written Work

## Public Lectures

CW 78    Anthroposophy, Its Roots of Knowledge and Fruits for Life
CW 79    The Reality of the Higher Worlds
CW 80    Public lectures in various cities, 1922
CW 81    Renewal-Impulses for Culture and Science–Berlin College Course
CW 82    So that the Human Being Can Become a Complete Human Being
CW 83    Western and Eastern World-Contrast. Paths to Understanding It through Anthroposophy
CW 84    What Did the Goetheanum Intend and What Should Anthroposophy Do?

## Lectures to the Members of the Anthroposophical Society

CW 88    Concerning the Astral World and Devachan
CW 89    Consciousness–Life–Form. Fundamental Principles of a Spiritual-Scientific Cosmology
CW 90    Participant Notes from the Lectures during the Years 1903-1905
CW 91    Participant Notes from the Lectures during the Years 1903-1905
CW 92    The Occult Truths of Ancient Myths and Sagas
CW 93    The Temple Legend and the Golden Legend
CW 93a    Fundamentals of Esotericism
CW 94    Cosmogony. Popular Occultism. The Gospel of John. The Theosophy in the Gospel of John
CW 95    At the Gates of Theosophy
CW 96    Origin-Impulses of Spiritual Science. Christian Esotericism in the Light of New Spirit-Knowledge
CW 97    The Christian Mystery
CW 98    Nature Beings and Spirit Beings – Their Effects in Our Visible World
CW 99    The Theosophy of the Rosicrucians
CW 100    Human Development and Christ-Knowledge
CW 101    Myths and Legends. Occult Signs and Symbols
CW 102    The Working into Human Beings by Spiritual Beings
CW 103    The Gospel of John
CW 104    The Apocalypse of John
CW 104a    From the Picture-Script of the Apocalypse of John
CW 105    Universe, Earth, the Human Being: Their Being and Development, as well as Their Reflection in the Connection between Egyptian Mythology and Modern Culture
CW 106    Egyptian Myths and Mysteries in Relation to the Active Spiritual Forces of the Present
CW 107    Spiritual-Scientific Knowledge of the Human Being
CW 108    Answering the Questions of Life and the World through Anthroposophy

CW 224     The Human Soul and its Connection with Divine-Spiritual Individualities. The Internalization of the Festivals of the Year

CW 225     Three Perspectives of Anthroposophy. Cultural Phenomena observed from a Spiritual-Scientific Perspective

CW 226     Human Being, Human Destiny, and World Development

CW 227     Initiation-Knowledge

CW 228     Science of Initiation and Knowledge of the Stars. The Human Being in the Past, the Present, and the Future from the Viewpoint of the Development of Consciousness

CW 229     The Experiencing of the Course of the Year in Four Cosmic Imaginations

CW 230     The Human Being as Harmony of the Creative, Building, and Formative World-Word

CW 231     The Supersensible Human Being, Understood Anthroposophically

CW 232     The Forming of the Mysteries

CW 233     World History Illuminated by Anthroposophy and as the Foundation for Knowledge of the Human Spirit

CW 233a     Mystery Sites of the Middle Ages: Rosicrucianism and the Modern Initiation-Principle. The Festival of Easter as Part of the History of the Mysteries of Humanity

CW 234     Anthroposophy. A Summary after 21 Years

CW 235     Esoteric Observations of Karmic Relationships in 6 Volumes, Vol. 1

CW 236     Esoteric Observations of Karmic Relationships in 6 Volumes, Vol. 2

CW 237     Esoteric Observations of Karmic Relationships in 6 Volumes, Vol. 3: The Karmic Relationships of the Anthroposophical Movement

CW 238     Esoteric Observations of Karmic Relationships in 6 Volumes, Vol. 4: The Spiritual Life of the Present in Relationship to the Anthroposophical Movement

CW 239     Esoteric Observations of Karmic Relationships in 6 Volumes, Vol. 5

CW 240     Esoteric Observations of Karmic Relationships in 6 Volumes, Vol. 6

CW 243     The Consciousness of the Initiate

CW 245     Instructions for an Esoteric Schooling

CW 250     The Building-Up of the Anthroposophical Society. From the Beginning to the Outbreak of the First World War

CW 251     The History of the Goetheanum Building-Association

CW 252     Life in the Anthroposophical Society from the First World War to the Burning of the First Goetheanum

CW 253     The Problems of Living Together in the Anthroposophical Society. On the Dornach Crisis of 1915. With Highlights on Swedenborg's Clairvoyance, the Views of Freudian Psychoanalysts, and the Concept of Love in Relation to Mysticism

CW 267    Soul-Exercises: Vol. 1: Exercises with Word and Image
          Meditations for the Methodological Development of Higher
          Powers of Knowledge, 1904-1924
CW 268    Soul-Exercises: Vol. 2: Mantric Verses, 1903-1925
CW 269    Ritual Texts for the Celebration of the Free Christian Religious
          Instruction. The Collected Verses for Teachers and Students of
          the Waldorf School
CW 270    Esoteric Instructions for the First Class of the School for Spiritual
          Science at the Goetheanum 1924, 4 Volumes
CW 271    Art and Knowledge of Art. Foundations of a New Aesthetic
CW 272    Spiritual-Scientific Commentary on Goethe's "Faust" in Two
          Volumes. Vol. 1: Faust, the Striving Human Being
CW 273    Spiritual-Scientific Commentary on Goethe's "Faust" in Two
          Volumes. Vol. 2: The Faust-Problem
CW 274    Addresses for the Christmas Plays from the Old Folk Traditions
CW 275    Art in the Light of Mystery-Wisdom
CW 276    The Artistic in Its Mission in the World. The Genius of
          Language. The World of the Self-Revealing Radiant Appearances
          – Anthroposophy and Art. Anthroposophy and Poetry
CW 277    Eurythmy. The Revelation of the Speaking Soul
CW 277a   The Origin and Development of Eurythmy
CW 278    Eurythmy as Visible Song
CW 279    Eurythmy as Visible Speech
CW 280    The Method and Nature of Speech Formation
CW 281    The Art of Recitation and Declamation
CW 282    Speech Formation and Dramatic Art
CW 283    The Nature of Things Musical and the Experience of Tone in the
          Human Being
CW284/285 Images of Occult Seals and Pillars. The Munich Congress of
          Whitsun 1907 and Its Consequences
CW 286    Paths to a New Style of Architecture. "And the Building Becomes
          Human"
CW 287    The Building at Dornach as a Symbol of Historical Becoming
          and an Artistic Transformation Impulse
CW 288    Style-Forms in the Living Organic
CW 289    The Building-Idea of the Goetheanum: Lectures with Slides from
          the Years 1920-1921
CW 290    The Building-Idea of the Goetheanum: Lectures with Slides from
          the Years 1920-1921
CW 291    The Nature of Colors
CW 291a   Knowledge of Colors. Supplementary Volume to "The Nature of
          Colors"
CW 292    Art History as Image of Inner Spiritual Impulses

# SIGNIFICANT EVENTS
## IN THE LIFE OF RUDOLF STEINER

1829:   June 23: birth of Johann Steiner (1829-1910)—Rudolf Steiner's father—in Geras, Lower Austria.

1834:   May 8: birth of Franciska Blie (1834-1918)—Rudolf Steiner's mother—in Horn, Lower Austria. "My father and mother were both children of the glorious Lower Austrian forest district north of the Danube."

1860:   May 16: marriage of Johann Steiner and Franciska Blie.

1861:   February 25: birth of *Rudolf Joseph Lorenz Steiner* in Kraljevec, Croatia, near the border with Hungary, where Johann Steiner works as a telegrapher for the South Austria Railroad. Rudolf Steiner is baptized two days later, February 27, the date usually given as his birthday.

1862:   Summer: the family moves to Mödling, Lower Austria.

1863:   The family moves to Pottschach, Lower Austria, near the Styrian border, where Johann Steiner becomes stationmaster. "The view stretched to the mountains...majestic peaks in the distance and the sweet charm of nature in the immediate surroundings."

1864:   November 15: birth of Rudolf Steiner's sister, Leopoldine (d. November 1, 1927). She will become a seamstress and live with her parents for the rest of her life.

1866:   July 28: birth of Rudolf Steiner's deaf-mute brother, Gustav (d. May 1, 1941).

1867:   Rudolf Steiner enters the village school. Following a disagreement between his father and the schoolmaster, whose wife falsely accused the boy of causing a commotion, Rudolf Steiner is taken out of school and taught at home.

1868:   A critical experience. Unknown to the family, an aunt dies in a distant town. Sitting in the station waiting room, Rudolf Steiner sees her "form," which speaks to him, asking for help. "Beginning with this experience, a new soul life began in the boy, one in which not only the outer trees and mountains spoke to him, but also the worlds that lay behind them. From this moment on, the boy began to live with the spirits of nature...."

1869:   The family moves to the peaceful, rural village of Neudorfl, near Wiener-Neustadt in present-day Hungary. Rudolf Steiner attends the village school. Because of the "unorthodoxy" of his writing and spelling, he has to do "extra lessons."

1870:   Through a book lent to him by his tutor, he discovers geometry: "To grasp something purely in the spirit brought me inner happiness. I know that I first learned happiness through geometry." The same tutor allows him to draw, while other students still struggle with their reading and writing. "An artistic element" thus enters his education.

1871: Though his parents are not religious, Rudolf Steiner becomes a "church child," a favorite of the priest, who was "an exceptional character." "Up to the age of ten or eleven, among those I came to know, he was far and away the most significant." Among other things, he introduces Steiner to Copernican, heliocentric cosmology. As an altar boy, Rudolf Steiner serves at Masses, funerals, and Corpus Christi processions. At year's end, after an incident in which he escapes a thrashing, his father forbids him to go to church.

1872: Rudolf Steiner transfers to grammar school in Wiener-Neustadt, a five-mile walk from home, which must be done in all weathers.

1873-75: Through his teachers and on his own, Rudolf Steiner has many wonderful experiences with science and mathematics. Outside school, he teaches himself analytic geometry, trigonometry, differential equations, and calculus.

1876: Rudolf Steiner begins tutoring other students. He learns bookbinding from his father. He also teaches himself stenography.

1877: Rudolf Steiner discovers Kant's *Critique of Pure Reason*, which he reads and rereads. He also discovers and reads von Rotteck's *World History*.

1878: He studies extensively in contemporary psychology and philosophy.

1879: Rudolf Steiner graduates from high school with honors. His father is transferred to Inzersdorf, near Vienna. He uses his first visit to Vienna "to purchase a great number of philosophy books"—Kant, Fichte, Schelling, and Hegel, as well as numerous histories of philosophy. His aim: to find a path from the "I" to nature.

October 1879-1883: Rudolf Steiner attends the Technical College in Vienna—to study mathematics, chemistry, physics, mineralogy, botany, zoology, biology, geology, and mechanics—with a scholarship. He also attends lectures in history and literature, while avidly reading philosophy on his own. His two favorite professors are Karl Julius Schröer (German language and literature) and Edmund Reitlinger (physics). He also audits lectures by Robert Zimmerman on aesthetics and Franz Brentano on philosophy. During this year he begins his friendship with Moritz Zitter (1861-1921), who will help support him financially when he is in Berlin.

1880: Rudolf Steiner attends lectures on Schiller and Goethe by Karl Julius Schröer, who becomes his mentor. Also "through a remarkable combination of circumstances," he meets Felix Koguzki, an "herb gatherer" and healer, who could "see deeply into the secrets of nature." Rudolf Steiner will meet and study with this "emissary of the Master" throughout his time in Vienna.

1881: January: "… I didn't sleep a wink. I was busy with philosophical problems until about 12:30 a.m. Then, finally, I threw myself down on my couch. All my striving during the previous year had been to research whether the following statement by Schelling was true or not: *Within everyone dwells a secret, marvelous capacity to draw back from the stream of time—out of the self clothed in all that comes to us from outside—into our innermost being and there, in the immutable form of the Eternal, to look into ourselves.* I believe, and I am still quite certain of it, that I discovered this capacity in myself; I had long had an inkling of it. Now the whole of idealist philosophy stood before me in modified form. What's a sleepless night compared to that!"

Rudolf Steiner begins communicating with leading thinkers of the day, who send him books in return, which he reads eagerly.

July: "I am not one of those who dives into the day like an animal in human form. I pursue a quite specific goal, an idealistic aim—knowledge of the truth! This cannot be done offhandedly. It requires the greatest striving in the world, free of all egotism, and equally of all resignation."

August: Steiner puts down on paper for the first time thoughts for a "Philosophy of Freedom." "The striving for the absolute: this human yearning is freedom." He also seeks to outline a "peasant philosophy," describing what the worldview of a "peasant"—one who lives close to the earth and the old ways—really is.

1881-1882: Felix Koguzki, the herb gatherer, reveals himself to be the envoy of another, higher initiatory personality, who instructs Rudolf Steiner to penetrate Fichte's philosophy and to master modern scientific thinking as a preparation for right entry into the spirit. This "Master" also teaches him the double (evolutionary and involutionary) nature of time.

1882: Through the offices of Karl Julius Schröer, Rudolf Steiner is asked by Joseph Kurschner to edit Goethe's scientific works for the *Deutschen National-Literatur* edition. He writes "A Possible Critique of Atomistic Concepts" and sends it to Friedrich Theodore Vischer.

1883: Rudolf Steiner completes his college studies and begins work on the Goethe project.

1884: First volume of Goethe's *Scientific Writings* (CW 1) appears (March). He lectures on Goethe and Lessing, and Goethe's approach to science. In July, he enters the household of Ladislaus and Pauline Specht as tutor to the four Specht boys. He will live there until 1890. At this time, he meets Josef Breuer (1842-1925), the coauthor with Sigmund Freud of *Studies in Hysteria*, who is the Specht family doctor.

1885: While continuing to edit Goethe's writings, Rudolf Steiner reads deeply in contemporary philosophy (Edouard von Hartmann, Johannes Volkelt, and Richard Wahle, among others).

1886: May: Rudolf Steiner sends Kurschner the manuscript of *Outlines of Goethe's Theory of Knowledge* (CW 2), which appears in October, and which he sends out widely. He also meets the poet Marie Eugenie Delle Grazie and writes "Nature and Our Ideals" for her. He attends her salon, where he meets many priests, theologians, and philosophers, who will become his friends. Meanwhile, the director of the Goethe Archive in Weimar requests his collaboration with the *Sophien* edition of Goethe's works, particularly the writings on color.

1887:   At the beginning of the year, Rudolf Steiner is very sick. As the year progresses and his health improves, he becomes increasingly "a man of letters," lecturing, writing essays, and taking part in Austrian cultural life. In August-September, the second volume of Goethe's *Scientific Writings* appears.

1888:   January-July: Rudolf Steiner assumes editorship of the "German Weekly" (*Deutsche Wochenschrift*). He begins lecturing more intensively, giving, for example, a lecture titled "Goethe as Father of a New Aesthetics." He meets and becomes soul friends with Friedrich Eckstein (1861-1939), a vegetarian, philosopher of symbolism, alchemist, and musician, who will introduce him to various spiritual currents (including Theosophy) and with whom he will meditate and interpret esoteric and alchemical texts.

1889:   Rudolf Steiner first reads Nietzsche (*Beyond Good and Evil*). He encounters Theosophy again and learns of Madame Blavatsky in the Theosophical circle around Marie Lang (1858-1934). Here he also meets well-known figures of Austrian life, as well as esoteric figures like the occultist Franz Hartman and Karl Leinigen-Billigen (translator of C.G. Harrison's *The Transcendental Universe*.) During this period, Steiner first reads A.P. Sinnett's *Esoteric Buddhism* and Mabel Collins's *Light on the Path*. He also begins traveling, visiting Budapest, Weimar, and Berlin (where he meets philosopher Edouard von Hartman).

1890:   Rudolf Steiner finishes volume 3 of Goethe's scientific writings. He begins his doctoral dissertation, which will become *Truth and Science* (CW 3). He also meets the poet and feminist Rosa Mayreder (1858-1938), with whom he can exchange his most intimate thoughts. In September, Rudolf Steiner moves to Weimar to work in the Goethe-Schiller Archive.

1891:   Volume 3 of the Kurschner edition of Goethe appears. Meanwhile, Rudolf Steiner edits Goethe's studies in mineralogy and scientific writings for the *Sophien* edition. He meets Ludwig Laistner of the Cotta Publishing Company, who asks for a book on the basic question of metaphysics. From this will result, ultimately, *The Philosophy of Freedom* (CW 4), which will be published not by Cotta but by Emil Felber. In October, Rudolf Steiner takes the oral exam for a doctorate in philosophy, mathematics, and mechanics at Rostock University, receiving his doctorate on the twenty-sixth. In November, he gives his first lecture on Goethe's "Fairy Tale" in Vienna.

1892:   Rudolf Steiner continues work at the Goethe-Schiller Archive and on his *Philosophy of Freedom*. *Truth and Science*, his doctoral dissertation, is published. Steiner undertakes to write introductions to books on Schopenhauer and Jean Paul for Cotta. At year's end, he finds lodging with Anna Eunike, née Schulz (1853-1911), a widow with four daughters and a son. He also develops a friendship with Otto Erich Hartleben (1864-1905) with whom he shares literary interests.

1893:  Rudolf Steiner begins his habit of producing many reviews and articles. In March, he gives a lecture titled "Hypnotism, with Reference to Spiritism." In September, volume 4 of the Kurschner edition is completed. In November, *The Philosophy of Freedom* appears. This year, too, he meets John Henry Mackay (1864-1933), the anarchist, and Max Stirner, a scholar and biographer.

1894:  Rudolf Steiner meets Elisabeth Förster Nietzsche, the philosopher's sister, and begins to read Nietzsche in earnest, beginning with the as yet unpublished *Antichrist*. He also meets Ernst Haeckel (1834-1919). In the fall, he begins to write *Nietzsche, A Fighter against His Time* (CW 5).

1895:  May, *Nietzsche, A Fighter against His Time* appears.

1896:  January 22: Rudolf Steiner sees Friedrich Nietzsche for the first and only time. Moves between the Nietzsche and the Goethe-Schiller Archives, where he completes his work before year's end. He falls out with Elisabeth Förster Nietzsche, thus ending his association with the Nietzsche Archive.

1897:  Rudolf Steiner finishes the manuscript of *Goethe's Worldview* (CW 6). He moves to Berlin with Anna Eunike and begins editorship of the *Magazin fur Literatur*. From now on, Steiner will write countless reviews, literary and philosophical articles, and so on. He begins lecturing at the "Free Literary Society." In September, he attends the Zionist Congress in Basel. He sides with Dreyfus in the Dreyfus affair.

1898:  Rudolf Steiner is very active as an editor in the political, artistic, and theatrical life of Berlin. He becomes friendly with John Henry Mackay and poet Ludwig Jacobowski (1868-1900). He joins Jacobowski's circle of writers, artists, and scientists—"The Coming Ones" (*Die Kommenden*)—and contributes lectures to the group until 1903. He also lectures at the "League for College Pedagogy." He writes an article for Goethe's sesquicentennial, "Goethe's Secret Revelation," on the "Fairy Tale of the Green Snake and the Beautiful Lily."

1888-89:  "This was a trying time for my soul as I looked at Christianity. . . . I was able to progress only by contemplating, by means of spiritual perception, the evolution of Christianity . . . . Conscious knowledge of real Christianity began to dawn in me around the turn of the century. This seed continued to develop. My soul trial occurred shortly before the beginning of the twentieth century. It was decisive for my soul's development that I stood spiritually before the Mystery of Golgotha in a deep and solemn celebration of knowledge."

1899:  Rudolf Steiner begins teaching and giving lectures and lecture cycles at the Workers' College, founded by Wilhelm Liebknecht (1826-1900). He will continue to do so until 1904. Writes: *Literature and Spiritual Life in the Nineteenth Century; Individualism in Philosophy; Haeckel and His Opponents; Poetry in the Present;* and begins what will become (fifteen years later). *The Riddles of Philosophy* (CW 18). He also meets many artists and writers, including Käthe Kollwitz, Stefan

Zweig, and Rainer Maria Rilke. On October 31, he marries Anna Eunike.

1900:   "I thought that the turn of the century must bring humanity a new light. It seemed to me that the separation of human thinking and willing from the spirit had peaked. A turn or reversal of direction in human evolution seemed to me a necessity." Rudolf Steiner finishes *World and Life Views in the Nineteenth Century* (the second part of what will become *The Riddles of Philosophy*) and dedicates it to Ernst Haeckel. It is published in March. He continues lecturing at *Die Kommenden*, whose leadership he assumes after the death of Jacobowski. Also, he gives the Gutenberg Jubilee lecture before 7,000 typesetters and printers. In September, Rudolf Steiner is invited by Count and Countess Brockdorff to lecture in the Theosophical Library. His first lecture is on Nietzsche. His second lecture is titled "Goethe's Secret Revelation." October 6, he begins a lecture cycle on the mystics that will become *Mystics after Modernism* (CW 7). November-December: "Marie von Sivers appears in the audience...." Also in November, Steiner gives his first lecture at the Giordano Bruno Bund (where he will continue to lecture until May, 1905). He speaks on Bruno and modern Rome, focusing on the importance of the philosophy of Thomas Aquinas as monism.

1901:   In continual financial straits, Rudolf Steiner's early friends Moritz Zitter and Rosa Mayreder help support him. In October, he begins the lecture cycle *Christianity as Mystical Fact* (CW 8) at the Theosophical Library. In November, he gives his first "Theosophical lecture" on Goethe's "Fairy Tale" in Hamburg at the invitation of Wilhelm Hubbe-Schleiden. He also attends a tea to celebrate the founding of the Theosophical Society at Count and Countess Brockdorff's. He gives a lecture cycle, "From Buddha to Christ," for the circle of the *Kommenden*. November 17, Marie von Sivers asks Rudolf Steiner if Theosophy does not need a Western-Christian spiritual movement (to complement Theosophy's Eastern emphasis). "The question was posed. Now, following spiritual laws, I could begin to give an answer...." In December, Rudolf Steiner writes his first article for a Theosophical publication. At year's end, the Brockdorffs and possibly Wilhelm Hubbe-Schleiden ask Rudolf Steiner to join the Theosophical Society and undertake the leadership of the German section. Rudolf Steiner agrees, on the condition that Marie von Sivers (then in Italy) work with him.

1902:   Beginning in January, Rudolf Steiner attends the opening of the Workers' School in Spandau with Rosa Luxemberg (1870-1919). January 17, Rudolf Steiner joins the Theosophical Society. In April, he is asked to become general secretary of the German Section of the Theosophical Society, and works on preparations for its founding. In July, he visits London for a Theosophical congress. He meets Bertram

Keightly, G.R.S. Mead, A.P. Sinnett, and Annie Besant, among others. In September, *Christianity as Mystical Fact* appears. In October, Rudolf Steiner gives his first public lecture on Theosophy ("Monism and Theosophy") to about three hundred people at the Giordano Bruno Bund. On October 19-21, the German Section of the Theosophical Society has its first meeting; Rudolf Steiner is the general secretary, and Annie Besant attends. Steiner lectures on practical karma studies. On October 23, Annie Besant inducts Rudolf Steiner into the Esoteric School of the Theosophical Society. On October 25, Steiner begins a weekly series of lectures: "The Field of Theosophy." During this year, Rudolf Steiner also first meets Ita Wegman (1876-1943), who will become his close collaborator in his final years.

1903: Rudolf Steiner holds about 300 lectures and seminars. In May, the first issue of the periodical *Luzifer* appears. In June, Rudolf Steiner visits London for the first meeting of the Federation of the European Sections of the Theosophical Society, where he meets Colonel Olcott. He begins to write *Theosophy* (CW 9).

1904: Rudolf Steiner continues lecturing at the Workers' College and elsewhere (about 90 lectures), while lecturing intensively all over Germany among Theosophists (about a 140 lectures). In February, he meets Carl Unger (1878-1929), who will become a member of the board of the Anthroposophical Society (1913). In March, he meets Michael Bauer (1871-1929), a Christian mystic, who will also be on the board. In May, *Theosophy* appears, with the dedication: "To the spirit of Giordano Bruno." Rudolf Steiner and Marie von Sivers visit London for meetings with Annie Besant. June: Rudolf Steiner and Marie von Sivers attend the meeting of the Federation of European Sections of the Theosophical Society in Amsterdam. In July, Steiner begins the articles in *Luzifer-Gnosis* that will become *How to Know Higher Worlds* (CW 10) and *Cosmic Memory* (CW 11). In September, Annie Besant visits Germany. In December, Steiner lectures on Freemasonry. He mentions the High Grade Masonry derived from John Yarker and represented by Theodore Reuss and Karl Kellner as a blank slate "into which a good image could be placed."

1905: This year, Steiner ends his non-Theosophical lecturing activity. Supported by Marie von Sivers, his Theosophical lecturing—both in public and in the Theosophical Society—increases significantly: "The German Theosophical Movement is of exceptional importance." Steiner recommends reading, among others, Fichte, Jacob Boehme, and Angelus Silesius. He begins to introduce Christian themes into Theosophy. He also begins to work with doctors (Felix Peipers and Ludwig Noll). In July, he is in London for the Federation of European Sections, where he attends a lecture by Annie Besant: "I have seldom seen Mrs. Besant speak in so inward and heartfelt a manner...." "Through Mrs. Besant I have found the way to H.P. Blavatsky."

September to October, he gives a course of thirty-one lectures for a small group of esoteric students. In October, the annual meeting of the German Section of the Theosophical Society, which still remains very small, takes place. Rudolf Steiner reports membership has risen from 121 to 377 members. In November, seeking to establish esoteric "continuity," Rudolf Steiner and Marie von Sivers participate in a "Memphis-Misraim" Masonic ceremony. They pay forty-five marks for membership. "Yesterday, you saw how little remains of former esoteric institutions." "We are dealing only with a 'framework'… for the present, nothing lies behind it. The occult powers have completely withdrawn."

1906: Expansion of Theosophical work. Rudolf Steiner gives about 245 lectures, only 44 of which take place in Berlin. Cycles are given in Paris, Leipzig, Stuttgart, and Munich. Esoteric work also intensifies. Rudolf Steiner begins writing *An Outline of Esoteric Science* (CW 13). In January, Rudolf Steiner receives permission (a patent) from the Great Orient of the Scottish A & A Thirty-Three Degree Rite of the Order of the Ancient Freemasons of the Memphis-Misraim Rite to direct a chapter under the name "Mystica Aeterna." This will become the "Cognitive Cultic Section" (also called "Misraim Service") of the Esoteric School. (See: *From the History and Contents of the Cognitive Cultic Section* (CW 264). During this time, Steiner also meets Albert Schweitzer. In May, he is in Paris, where he visits Edouard Schuré. Many Russians attend his lectures (including Konstantin Balmont, Dimitri Mereszkovski, Zinaida Hippius, and Maximilian Woloshin). He attends the General Meeting of the European Federation of the Theosophical Society, at which Col. Olcott is present for the last time. He spends the year's end in Venice and Rome, where he writes and works on his translation of H.P. Blavatsky's *Key to Theosophy*.

1907: Further expansion of the German Theosophical Movement according to the Rosicrucian directive to "introduce spirit into the world"—in education, in social questions, in art, and in science. In February, Col. Olcott dies in Adyar. Before he dies, Olcott indicates that "the Masters" wish Annie Besant to succeed him: much politicking ensues. Rudolf Steiner supports Besant's candidacy. April-May: preparations for the Congress of the Federation of European Sections of the Theosophical Society—the great, watershed Whitsun "Munich Congress," attended by Annie Besant and others. Steiner decides to separate Eastern and Western (Christian-Rosicrucian) esoteric schools. He takes his esoteric school out of the Theosophical Society (Besant and Rudolf Steiner are "in harmony" on this). Steiner makes his first lecture tours to Austria and Hungary. That summer, he is in Italy. In September, he visits Edouard Schuré, who will write the introduction to the French edition of *Christianity as Mystical Fact* in Barr, Alsace. Rudolf Steiner writes the autobiographical statement known as the "Barr Document." In *Luzifer–Gnosis*, "The Education of the Child" appears.

1908:  The movement grows (membership: 1150). Lecturing expands. Steiner makes his first extended lecture tour to Holland and Scandinavia, as well as visits to Naples and Sicily. Themes: St. John's Gospel, the Apocalypse, Egypt, science, philosophy, and logic. *Luzifer-Gnosis* ceases publication. In Berlin, Marie von Sivers (with Johanna Mücke (1864-1949) forms the *Philosophisch-Theosophisch* (after 1915 *Philosophisch-Anthroposophisch*) *Verlag* to publish Steiner's work. Steiner gives lecture cycles titled *The Gospel of St. John* (CW 103) and *The Apocalypse* (104).

1909:  *An Outline of Esoteric Science* appears. Lecturing and travel continues. Rudolf Steiner's spiritual research expands to include the polarity of Lucifer and Ahriman; the work of great individualities in history; the Maitreya Buddha and the Bodhisattvas; spiritual economy (CW 109); the work of the spiritual hierarchies in heaven and on Earth (CW 110). He also deepens and intensifies his research into the Gospels, giving lectures on the Gospel of St. Luke (CW 114) with the first mention of two Jesus children. Meets and becomes friends with Christian Morgenstern (1871-1914). In April, he lays the foundation stone for the Malsch model—the building that will lead to the first Goetheanum. In May, the International Congress of the Federation of European Sections of the Theosophical Society takes place in Budapest. Rudolf Steiner receives the Subba Row medal for *How to Know Higher Worlds*. During this time, Charles W. Leadbeater discovers Jiddu Krishnamurti (1895-1986) and proclaims him the future "world teacher," the bearer of the Maitreya Buddha and the "reappearing Christ." In October, Steiner delivers seminal lectures on "anthroposophy," which he will try, unsuccessfully, to rework over the next years into the unfinished work, *Anthroposophy (A Fragment)* (CW 45).

1910:  New themes: *The Reappearance of Christ in the Etheric* (CW 118); *The Fifth Gospel; The Mission of Folk Souls* (CW 121); *Occult History* (CW 126); the evolving development of etheric cognitive capacities. Rudolf Steiner continues his Gospel research with *The Gospel of St. Matthew* (CW 123). In January, his father dies. In April, he takes a month-long trip to Italy, including Rome, Monte Cassino, and Sicily. He also visits Scandinavia again. July-August, he writes the first mystery drama, *The Portal of Initiation* (CW 14). In November, he gives "psychosophy" lectures. In December, he submits "On the Psychological Foundations and Epistemological Framework of Theosophy" to the International Philosophical Congress in Bologna.

1911:  The crisis in the Theosophical Society deepens. In January, "The Order of the Rising Sun," which will soon become "The Order of the Star in the East," is founded for the coming world teacher, Krishnamurti. At the same time, Marie von Sivers, Rudolf Steiner's coworker, falls ill. Fewer lectures are given, but important new ground is broken. In Prague, in March, Steiner meets Franz Kafka (1883-1924) and Hugo Bergmann (1883-1975). In April, he delivers his paper to the

Philosophical Congress. He writes the second mystery drama, *The Soul's Probation* (CW 14). Also, while Marie von Sivers is convalescing, Rudolf Steiner begins work on *Calendar 1912/1913*, which will contain the "Calendar of the Soul" meditations. On March 19, Anna (Eunike) Steiner dies. In September, Rudolf Steiner visits Einsiedeln, birthplace of Paracelsus. In December, Friedrich Rittelmeyer, future founder of the Christian Community, meets Rudolf Steiner. The *Johannes-Bauverein*, the "building committee," which would lead to the first Goetheanum (first planned for Munich), is also founded, and a preliminary committee for the founding of an independent association is created that, in the following year, will become the Anthroposophical Society. Important lecture cycles include *Occult Physiology* (CW 128); *Wonders of the World* (CW 129); *From Jesus to Christ* (CW 131). Other themes: esoteric Christianity; Christian Rosenkreutz; the spiritual guidance of humanity; the sense world and the world of the spirit.

1912:   Despite the ongoing, now increasing crisis in the Theosophical Society, much is accomplished: *Calendar 1912/1913* is published; eurythmy is created; both the third mystery drama, *The Guardian of the Threshold* (CW 14) and *A Way of Self-Knowledge* (CW 16) are written. New (or renewed) themes included life between death and rebirth and karma and reincarnation. Other lecture cycles: *Spiritual Beings in the Heavenly Bodies and the Kingdoms of Nature* (CW 136); *The Human Being in the Light of Occultism, Theosophy, and Philosophy* (CW 137); *The Gospel of St. Mark* (CW 139); and *The Bhagavad Gita and the Epistles of Paul* (CW 142). On May 8, Rudolf Steiner celebrates White Lotus Day, H.P. Blavatsky's death day, which he had faithfully observed for the past decade, for the last time. In August, Rudolf Steiner suggests the "independent association" be called the "Anthroposophical Society." In September, the first eurythmy course takes place. In October, Rudolf Steiner declines recognition of a Theosophical Society lodge dedicated to the Star of the East and decides to expel all Theosophical Society members belonging to the order. Also, with Marie von Sivers, he first visits Dornach, near Basel, Switzerland, and they stand on the hill where the Goetheanum will be. In November, a Theosophical Society lodge is opened by direct mandate from Adyar (Annie Besant). In December, a meeting of the German section occurs at which it is decided that belonging to the Order of the Star of the East is incompatible with membership in the Theosophical Society. December 28: informal founding of the Anthroposophical Society in Berlin.

1913:   Expulsion of the German section from the Theosophical Society. February 2-3: Foundation meeting of the Anthroposophical Society. Board members include: Marie von Sivers, Michael Bauer, and Carl Unger. September 20: Laying of the foundation stone for the *Johannes Bau* (Goetheanum) in Dornach. Building begins immediately. The third mystery drama, *The Soul's Awakening* (CW 14), is completed.

Also: *The Threshold of the Spiritual World* (CW 147). Lecture cycles include: *The Bhagavad Gita and the Epistles of Paul* and *The Esoteric Meaning of the Bhagavad Gita* (CW 146), which the Russian philosopher Nikolai Berdyaev attends; *The Mysteries of the East and of Christianity* (CW 144); *The Effects of Esoteric Development* (CW 145); and *The Fifth Gospel* (CW 148). In May, Rudolf Steiner is in London and Paris, where anthroposophical work continues.

1914: Building continues on the *Johannes Bau* (Goetheanum) in Dornach, with artists and coworkers from seventeen nations. The general assembly of the Anthroposophical Society takes place. In May, Rudolf Steiner visits Paris, as well as Chartres Cathedral. June 28: assassination in Sarajevo ("Now the catastrophe has happened!"). August 1: War is declared. Rudolf Steiner returns to Germany from Dornach—he will travel back and forth. He writes the last chapter of *The Riddles of Philosophy*. Lecture cycles include: *Human and Cosmic Thought* (CW 151); *Inner Being of Humanity between Death and a New Birth* (CW 153); *Occult Reading and Occult Hearing* (CW 156). December 24: marriage of Rudolf Steiner and Marie von Sivers.

1915: Building continues. Life after death becomes a major theme, also art. Writes: *Thoughts during a Time of War* (CW 24). Lectures include: *The Secret of Death* (CW 159); *The Uniting of Humanity through the Christ Impulse* (CW 165).

1916: Rudolf Steiner begins work with Edith Maryon (1872-1924) on the sculpture "The Representative of Humanity" ("The Group"—Christ, Lucifer, and Ahriman). He also works with the alchemist Alexander von Bernus on the quarterly *Das Reich*. He writes *The Riddle of Humanity* (CW 20). Lectures include: *Necessity and Freedom in World History and Human Action* (CW 166); *Past and Present in the Human Spirit* (CW 167); *The Karma of Vocation* (CW 172); *The Karma of Untruthfulness* (CW 173).

1917: Russian Revolution. The U.S. enters the war. Building continues. Rudolf Steiner delineates the idea of the "threefold nature of the human being" (in a public lecture March 15) and the "threefold nature of the social organism" (hammered out in May-June with the help of Otto von Lerchenfeld and Ludwig Polzer-Hoditz in the form of two documents titled *Memoranda*, which were distributed in high places). August-September: Rudolf Steiner writes *The Riddles of the Soul* (CW 20). Also: commentary on "The Chemical Wedding of Christian Rosenkreutz" for Alexander Bernus (*Das Reich*). Lectures include: *The Karma of Materialism* (CW 176); *The Spiritual Background of the Outer World: The Fall of the Spirits of Darkness* (CW 177).

1918: March 18: peace treaty of Brest-Litovsk—"Now everything will truly enter chaos! What is needed is cultural renewal." June: Rudolf Steiner visits Karlstein (Grail) Castle outside Prague. Lecture cycle: *From Symptom to Reality in Modern History* (CW 185). In mid-November,

Emil Molt, of the Waldorf-Astoria Cigarette Company, has the idea of founding a school for his workers' children.

1919: Focus on the threefold social organism: tireless travel, countless lectures, meetings, and publications. At the same time, a new public stage of Anthroposophy emerges as cultural renewal begins. The coming years will see initiatives in pedagogy, medicine, pharmacology, and agriculture. January 27: threefold meeting: " We must first of all, with the money we have, found free schools that can bring people what they need." February: first public eurythmy performance in Zurich. Also: "Appeal to the German People" (CW 24), circulated March 6 as a newspaper insert. In April, *Toward Social Renewal* (CW 23)—"perhaps the most widely read of all books on politics appearing since the war"—appears. Rudolf Steiner is asked to undertake the "direction and leadership" of the school founded by the Waldorf-Astoria Company. Rudolf Steiner begins to talk about the "renewal" of education. May 30: a building is selected and purchased for the future Waldorf School. August-September, Rudolf Steiner gives a lecture course for Waldorf teachers, *The Foundations of Human Experience (Study of Man)* (CW 293). September 7: Opening of the first Waldorf School. December (into January): first science course, the *Light Course* (CW 320).

1920: The Waldorf School flourishes. New threefold initiatives. Founding of limited companies *Der Kommenden Tag* and *Futurum A.G.* to infuse spiritual values into the economic realm. Rudolf Steiner also focuses on the sciences. Lectures: *Introducing Anthroposophical Medicine* (CW 312); *The Warmth Course* (CW 321); *The Boundaries of Natural Science* (CW 322); *The Redemption of Thinking* (CW 74). February: Johannes Werner Klein—later a cofounder of the Christian Community—asks Rudolf Steiner about the possibility of a "religious renewal," a "Johannine church." In March, Rudolf Steiner gives the first course for doctors and medical students. In April, a divinity student asks Rudolf Steiner a second time about the possibility of religious renewal. September 27-October 16: anthroposophical "university course." December: lectures titled *The Search for the New Isis* (CW 202).

1921: Rudolf Steiner continues his intensive work on cultural renewal, including the uphill battle for the threefold social order. "University" arts, scientific, theological, and medical courses include: *The Astronomy Course* (CW 323); *Observation, Mathematics, and Scientific Experiment* (CW 324); the *Second Medical Course* (CW 313); *Color.* In June and September-October, Rudolf Steiner also gives the first two "priests' courses" (CW 342 and 343). The "youth movement" gains momentum. Magazines are founded: *Die Drei* (January), and—under the editorship of Albert Steffen (1884-1963)—the weekly, *Das Goetheanum* (August). In February-March, Rudolf Steiner takes his first trip outside Germany since the war (Holland). On April 7, Steiner receives a letter regarding "religious renewal," and May 22-23, he agrees to address the question in a practical way. In June, the Klinical-Therapeutic Institute opens in Arlesheim under the direction of Dr. Ita Wegman. In August, the Chemical-Pharmaceutical Laboratory opens in Arlesheim (Oskar Schmiedel and Ita Wegman, directors). The Clinical Therapeutic Institute is inaugurated in Stuttgart (Dr. Ludwig Noll, director); also the Research Laboratory in Dornach (Ehrenfried Pfeiffer and Gunther Wachsmuth, directors). In November-December, Rudolf Steiner visits Norway.

1922:  The first half of the year involves very active public lecturing (thousands attend); in the second half, Rudolf Steiner begins to withdraw and turn toward the Society—"The Society is asleep." It is "too weak" to do what is asked of it. The businesses—*Die Kommenden Tag* and *Futura A.G.*—fail. In January, with the help of an agent, Steiner undertakes a twelve-city German tour, accompanied by eurythmy performances. In two weeks he speaks to more than 2,000 people. In April, he gives a "university course" in The Hague. He also visits England. In June, he is in Vienna for the East-West Congress. In August-September, he is back in England for the Oxford Conference on Education. Returning to Dornach, he gives the lectures *Philosophy, Cosmology, and Religion* (CW 215), and gives the third priest's course (CW 344). On September 16, The Christian Community is founded. In October-November, Steiner is in Holland and England. He also speaks to the youth: *The Youth Course* (CW 217). In December, Steiner gives lectures titled *The Origins of Natural Science* (CW 326), and *Humanity and the World of Stars: The Spiritual Communion of Humanity* (CW 219). December 31: Fire at the Goetheanum, which is destroyed.

1923:  Despite the fire, Rudolf Steiner continues his work unabated. A very hard year. Internal dispersion, dissension, and apathy abound. There is conflict—between old and new visions—within the society. A wake-up call is needed, and Rudolf Steiner responds with renewed lecturing vitality. His focus: the spiritual context of human life; initiation science; the course of the year; and community building. As a foundation for an artistic school, he creates a series of pastel sketches. Lecture cycles: *The Anthroposophical Movement; Initiation Science* (CW 227) (in England at the Penmaenmawr Summer School); *The Four Seasons and the Archangels* (CW 229); *Harmony of the Creative Word* (CW 230); *The Supersensible Human* (CW 231), given in Holland for the founding of the Dutch society. On November 10, in response to the failed Hitler-Ludendorf putsch in Munich, Steiner closes his Berlin residence and moves the *Philosophisch-Anthroposophisch Verlag* (Press) to Dornach. On December 9, Steiner begins the serialization of his *Autobiography: The Course of My Life* (CW 28) in *Das Goetheanum*. It will continue to appear weekly, without a break, until his death. Late December-early January: Rudolf Steiner refounds the Anthroposophical Society (about 12,000 members internationally) and takes over its leadership. The new board members are: Marie Steiner, Ita Wegman, Albert Steffen, Elizabeth Vreede, and Guenther Wachsmuth. (See *The Christmas Meeting for the Founding of the General Anthroposophical Society* (CW 260). Accompanying lectures: *Mystery Knowledge and Mystery Centers* (CW 232); *World History in the Light of Anthroposophy* (CW 233). December 25: the Foundation Stone is laid (in the hearts of members) in the form of the "Foundation Stone Meditation."

1924: January 1: having founded the Anthroposophical Society and taken over its leadership, Rudolf Steiner has the task of "reforming" it. The process begins with a weekly newssheet ("What's Happening in the Anthroposophical Society") in which Rudolf Steiner's "Letters to Members" and "Anthroposophical Leading Thoughts" appear (CW 26). The next step is the creation of a new esoteric class, the "first class" of the "University of Spiritual Science" (which was to have been followed, had Rudolf Steiner lived longer, by two more advanced classes). Then comes a new language for Anthroposophy—practical, phenomenological, and direct; and Rudolf Steiner creates the model for the second Goetheanum. He begins the series of extensive "karma" lectures (CW 235-40); and finally, responding to needs, he creates two new initiatives: biodynamic agriculture and curative education. After the middle of the year, rumors begin to circulate regarding Steiner's health. Lectures: January-February, *Anthroposophy* (CW 234); February: *Tone Eurythmy* (CW 278); June: *The Agriculture Course* (CW 327); June-July: Speech [?] Eurythmy (CW 279); *Curative Education* (CW 317); August: (England, "Second International Summer School"), *Initiation Consciousness: True and False Paths in Spiritual Investigation* (CW 243); September: *Pastoral Medicine* (CW 318). On September 26, for the first time, Rudolf Steiner cancels a lecture. On September 28, he gives his last lecture. On September 29, he withdraws to his studio in the carpenter's shop; now he is definitively ill. Cared for by Ita Wegman, he continues working, however, and writing the weekly installments of his *Autobiography* and *Letters to the Members/Leading Thoughts* (CW 26).

1925: Rudolf Steiner, while continuing to work, continues to weaken. He finishes *Extending Practical Medicine* (CW 27) with Ita Wegman. On March 30, around ten in the morning, Rudolf Steiner dies.

# INDEX